Praise for "Chopsticks in the Land of Cotton"

John Jung's third book about relatively undocumented aspects of Chinese American history is a solid, well-researched, and engagingly written study of the Chinese grocery stores in the Mississippi River Delta from their post-Civil War Reconstruction era beginnings to the present. Jung deftly demonstrates how these sojourners from the Guangdong province found their niche in a unique and challengingly complex social setting, rigidly stratified by race. They not only 'survived,' but overcame racism to prosper and eventually become valued members of their communities. After a thorough historical background that provides a framework needed to fully portray their difficult circumstances, the author examines both the sociological and psychological aspects of daily life for Chinese American grocery store families. As a Chinese American who grew up in the Deep South himself, John Jung has a degree of empathy that imbues *Chopsticks in the Land of Cotton* with an insight both in depth and breadth that is totally requisite for a study of this nature.

Mel Brown, *Chinese Heart of Texas, The San Antonio Community, 1875-1975; Editor, TexAsia, San Antonio's Asian Communities, 1978-2008.*

In *Chopsticks in The Land of Cotton*, John Jung has done it again! Plunging into the history of Chinese grocers in the Mississippi-Yazoo Delta, he traces their migration history, work, families, and social lives. His work is anchored in a creative mix of oral history, community historical documents and public records, and includes a generous fill of photos. As a study of the complexities of triangular race relations in the Jim Crow South, his work rivals James Loewen's classic study, *The Mississippi Chinese*.

Greg Robinson, *By Order of the President: FDR and the Internment of Japanese Americans* Harvard University Press, 2001; Co-Editor, *Mine Okubo: Following Her Own Road* University of Washington Press, 2008.

"Chopsticks" tells the story of yet one more example of Chinese tenacity in which John Jung traces the paths of pioneer Chinese immigrants in Mississippi as they moved from laborers to become successful grocery store merchants for decades with family members and relatives serving as the backbone. *"Chopsticks"* pays tribute to the resilience and "can-do" attitude of these enterprising entrepreneurs.

Sylvia Sun Minnick, *Sam Fow, The San Joaquin Chinese Legacy*

Chopsticks in the Land of Cotton explores aspects of Chinese settlement in the Mississippi Delta that earlier writings on the subject do not address in detail. Jung analyzes why grocery stores emerged as virtually the only occupation for Chinese in that area instead of farming and hand laundries. He examines the extensive kinship networking that brought male relatives and later whole families to this unlikely region for Chinese settlement. Jung's impressive book can be enjoyed by ordinary readers for its captivating stories and by scholars for its thorough research and analysis of sources.

Daniel Bronstein, *The Formation and Development of Chinese Communities in Atlanta, Augusta, And Savannah, Georgia: From Sojourners To Settlers, 1880-1965*

John Jung provides meticulous detail on a subject worth much greater examination: the Chinese grocery stores of the South. These grocery stores were the center of Chinese American family and commercial life in the South, including Texas and the Southwest, for at least half of the twentieth century. Jung illuminates every aspect of these grocery stores, which were as important to black neighborhoods as they were to the Chinese American families who ran them. Especially of interest is Jung's exploration of the relationships between Chinese Americans and African Americans, a topic distorted by the iconic images of more recent inter-ethnic conflicts. *Chopsticks* is a valuable contribution to Asian American history.

Irwin Tang, *Co-Author and Editor Asian Texans: Our Histories and Our Lives*

Chopsticks in the Land of Cotton

Lives of Mississippi Delta Chinese Grocers

John Jung

Yin & Yang Press

LCCN: 2007910365
ISBN 978-0-6151-8571-2

Jung, John, 1937-
Chopsticks in the Land of Cotton/ Lives of Mississippi Delta Chinese Grocers/
/John Jung

p. cm. (Chinese American history)
Includes bibliographical references and index.

Front Cover Design Consultant: Lauren Doege
Photographs
Top Row: Three Delta street scenes
Middle Row: Joe Gow Nue Grocery, Greenville
Bottom Row: (L-R) Sit and Seid family in Mee Jon store, Greenville
Joe Guay and son, Joe Ting, Greenville
Cotton pickers in the field

Back Cover Photographs:
Top Row (L-R): white plantation boss with workers;
A cotton coop store,
Street domino game
Middle Row (L-R): N. Gee Store, Lake Village, Ak;
Chinese Mission School Students, Cleveland
Quon family store, Moorhead
Bottom Row (L-R): Cotton hoers in the field;
Juke joint, black section, Clarksdale
Rex Colored Theater, Leland

Author, KTVU-TV Interview

Online Orders: www.lulu.com/chinesegrocery

Second Printing, Jan. 2009.

To
Honor
Pioneering
Chinese Grocery Families
Who Overcame Great Odds
With Resolve and Resourcefulness
To Provide for, Protect, and Preserve Family

Table of Contents

Foreword

Historian James Cobb describes the Mississippi River Delta as the most southern place on earth. It is an apt label for the alluvial plain created by the Mississippi River that covers the northwest portion of Mississippi and southeast Arkansas. But what makes the Delta unique is not its geography, but rather its social and cultural history.

The Mississippi River Delta has always been a land of contrasts. For late nineteenth-century and much of the twentieth century, large farms with antebellum-like homes dotted the Delta landscape. In their shadow were farm workers and sharecroppers eking out subsistence living. Apart from the farms, the small Delta towns relied on unspoken borders, usually railroads tracks to designate living space. There was a place for black and white and for the haves and the have-nots. There were social codes in place to ensure that borders of race and class were not violated. All knew their place, or so it seemed.

What no one could anticipate was that this seemingly intractable social order would be challenged, not by disenfranchised black citizens not yet to ready to embrace the modern civil rights struggle, but by a small group of Chinese who decided to make the Mississippi River Delta their home.

The labor conditions in the plantation south after the Civil War were unsettled. Would former slaves, now free blacks, remain and work in the fields? If so, at what price, both economically and socially? In the face of these questions, alternative labor seemed a viable solution for Delta land owners. One failed experiment was the recruitment of Chinese in small numbers to work on the farms. The Chinese found the arrangement unsatisfactory. They quickly turned away from farm labor to become merchants, an economic livelihood that better served their background and skills. They were joined by Chinese from other parts of the country who viewed a merchant life in the rural south as preferable to the prejudice and oppression they encountered in urban areas.

Thus was born the Chinese grocery store-a cultural icon that would dominate Delta towns throughout much of the twentieth century. The Chinese grocery store was almost always located in black neighborhoods, a strategic, but necessary decision. Blacks no longer relied on the plantation commissaries for goods, so the stores afforded an economic niche. Moreover, the establishment of such stores in white neighborhoods was socially unacceptable. The stores also served as living quarters for Chinese families, as they lived in the back/upstairs of the store. The decision to live in the stores made economic sense, but also reflected the total devotion of the Chinese to their stores.

The grocery stores afforded Chinese some economic success, and with it, the need to find their place in the Delta's dualistic social structure. The struggles they encountered in doing so and the eventual success they would achieve are a unique story. John Jung tells that story in *Chopsticks in the Land of Cotton*.

Two earlier books specifically on the Delta Chinese, *The Mississippi Chinese: Between Black and White* by James Loewen, and *Lotus Among the Magnolias: The Mississippi Chinese* by Robert Seto Quan, although valuable, reflected an academic research approach. *Chopsticks in the Land of Cotton* offers a different view, relying largely on the personal and poignant stories of the Chinese who faced the struggles of life and work in the Mississippi River Delta.

The challenges Chinese in the Delta faced were a microcosm of a national agenda dominated by prejudice and nativism. The apex of those movements is best reflected in passage of the Chinese Exclusion Act of 1882, legislation that placed the severest restrictions on Chinese migration. That such legislation was the first of its kind in the history of the country offers insight into the political landscape faced by Chinese in the United States in the late nineteenth and early twentieth centuries.

That political climate also extended to the Delta. Prejudice was a way of life in the south. Yet Delta Chinese faced a very different set of circumstances. There were no Chinese enclaves to offer sanctuary as existed in the large cities. Delta Chinese lived in their stores or in black neighborhoods and were small in number. They worked long hours in the stores and had no time for a life outside of work. Moreover, the racial ambiguity of being "between black and white" made important decisions of life such as education, church, medical services, marriage, and family life, continual struggles for Chinese.

The challenges the Delta Chinese faced and more importantly, the success they achieved in the face of those challenges is at the heart of *Chopsticks in the Land of Cotton.* Jung weaves together the narratives to tell their story.

Jung starts with the migration story. How did Chinese end up in a remote, rural area in the Deep South? What role did extended family and connections play in their arrival and their subsequent expansion? How much of a presence were they? How were they able to overcome the migration barriers put in place by the government? The book describes those multiple journeys ranging from the Guangdong Province in China, the gold mountains in California, and the sugarcane fields of Cuba and Louisiana.

Once settled in the Delta, the Chinese, many initially sojourners, decided to make it their permanent home. The cornerstone of their daily life was the grocery store where they live, worked, and raised a family. That life was characterized by total devotion to the success of the stores and the involvement of the entire family in the effort. Jung's chapter "Life in Chinese Grocery Stores" is a fascinating account of those efforts. Not only do readers have an opportunity to better understand the complexities of managing the stores, they can also appreciate the ancillary advantages that evolved out of those stores-the strong devotion to family that comes from a shared common goal and the ability to parent children who live and work in them.

Perhaps none of the challenges Delta Chinese faced were more daunting than schooling. Coming out of a Confucian tradition that acknowledged the hallowed importance of education, the Chinese families found the Delta an unfriendly place when it came to educating their children. The Mississippi Constitution mandated separate schools for black and white children. It failed to address a place for Chinese. Being neither black nor white, the question of where their children would attend school confronted families across the Delta. The black schools were grossly underfunded and inferior and the white schools were inaccessible. How Chinese dealt with this dilemma is troublesome given the inequities that existed, but also fascinating given the creativity the Chinese displayed in dealing with the decision. Jung's treatment of this challenge is insightful and once again displays the resiliency of the Chinese in responding to the myriad of problems they encountered as Delta citizens.

Jung also writes about similar access issues related to church attendance. Interestingly the schools proved to be a conduit to church. The white churches of the Delta saw the Chinese as a target for mission work and were anxious to find ways to partner toward that end. The evolution of residential schools for Chinese children was a response to the educational needs of the Chinese and the mission goals of the white churches. The Chinese also had an interest in social mobility within the white community and the church seemed a window to meet that objective. Jung's description of the events that led to a "church" solution is an excellent example of the ability of the Delta Chinese to find a merger of self interests in spite of a social power structure that was at cross purposes with their objectives.

Any analysis of southern history and politics addresses race. For the Delta Chinese, race relations were, as described by Jung, "a delicate situation." The Chinese lived and worked within the black community but wanted the favor of the white community. How that balancing act was achieved is explored by Jung through accounts of experiences by Delta Chinese who faced the complexities of race first-hand. The Chinese experienced such across a broad range of social areas such as school sports, hiring, and housing. Inevitably they found themselves confronted with racism, but also ever resilient in overcoming it. Jung's chapter on matters of segregation and race is especially poignant as it recounts incidents that remind the readers of the behavior of whites during this shameful era.

Jung's final chapters focus on the Chinese identity-what it means to be Chinese in the Delta-the most southern place on earth. Two elements stand out among many. First, the Chinese encountered enormous obstacles in their quest for economic and social legitimacy in the Delta. Second, they overcame those obstacles. Their legacy of accomplishment and achievement in the face of adversity is a model for all. Thanks to John Jung and his book *Chopsticks in the Land of Cotton* for sharing the powerful story of the Delta Chinese. The recognition is well deserved.

John Thornell
Rocky Mount, North Carolina
November, 2008

Preface

Attracted by the prospect of finding gold, Chinese immigrants from the impoverished Guangdong province of southeast China began to come to the United States and Canada in large numbers starting around the middle of the 19th century. Few succeeded in striking it rich, and most ended up engaged in backbreaking labor including railroad and levee construction, farming, fishing, and laundry work. Fueled by the threat of large supplies of cheap Chinese labor, white workers agitated for an end to their further entry, leading to the Chinese Exclusion Act in 1882.

Most Chinese entered from either coast, especially the Pacific, so it is somewhat surprising that a few settled in Arkansas and Mississippi along the Mississippi River. When outsiders think of Mississippi, they may think of cotton plantations, magnolias, slavery, or catfish but the thought of Chinese immigrants and their descendants would be an unlikely association. How did this incongruous combination of "chopsticks" and "cotton" come to be? *Chopsticks in the Land of Cotton* is the story of how these hardy immigrants found an economic niche in the racially segregated Delta. A distinct numerical minority, caught in the social structure of white supremacy and subjugated blacks, Chinese somehow found a way to survive economically while preserving their own ethnic identity.

The Delta afforded the Chinese immigrants of the late 1800s an opportunity to earn a living with more safety than in other regions where they were literally driven out. But, unlike their compatriots who settled on either coast near Chinatowns, Delta Chinese did not have access to the social and economic life of a densely populated Chinese community.

Delta Chinese, very few in number, were scattered over many small towns where almost all of them operated small grocery stores and markets in neighborhoods where poor black cotton plantation workers lived. *Chopsticks* first examines the factors that led the Chinese to assume this occupation, describes their working and living conditions, and analyzes how they countered the racial prejudices of the time and place. Of primary interest in the second half of the book is the story of the impact of their experiences in the grocery business on the lives of several cohorts of children, most U. S.-born, that came of age in the Delta during the mid- 20th century.

Understanding history is not unlike solving a mystery. We want to discover "truths," about the past. Who did what? When and where did it take place? Why, and how, did it happen? Since we were not present to witness these events, we have to rely on available evidence. However, many records of the past are absent, inaccurate, or incomplete. Personal testimonies and reminiscences, written or oral, can be vague, distorted, or inconsistent and difficult to corroborate or validate. Different observers may have made conflicting accounts for many reasons. Their own preconceptions and expectations may have affected what they saw and how they interpreted it. They may have examined different evidence or spoken to different people, some that embellished or suppressed memories and feelings. Gathering accurate and comprehensive historical data and making sense out of it is fraught with difficulty. It is small wonder that history is periodically rewritten or reinterpreted as perspectives change in the light of new evidence or subsequent events.

Roland Chow stimulated my initial interest in Delta Chinese history, encouraged me to pursue this project, and persuaded numerous contacts from the region to share memories with me. Bobby Joe Moon continually and promptly provided family history information, personal contacts, and strong conviction in the value of this work. Paul and Helen Wong graciously shared details of the history of their family ties with the venerable Joe Gow Nue Grocery in Greenville. Reverend Ted Shepherd, for many years a revered pastor at the Chinese Baptist Church in Greenville, kindly shared historical information and photographs about their church school. Henry Wong supplied details of the interconnections among several related families that led them to open grocery stores on the Arkansas side of the Delta. Gow Joe Low and Don Chu were also helpful. Emily Weaver, of the Oral History Archives at Delta State University provided access to valuable documents collected in 2000 from a score or more Delta Chinese that provided first-hand accounts of the experience of growing up in grocery stores.

Thanks for invaluable assistance are also due to many Delta Chinese who shared details from their personal experiences: Sung Gay Chow, Robert Chow, Bonnie Lew, Sam Sue, Frieda Quon, Audrey Sidney, C. W. Sidney May Jee, Peter Joe, Bobby Jue, Shirley Kwan, Sally and Gilroy Chow, Jack Joe, Dicksun Joe, Dickmun Joe, Hoover Lee, Leland Gion, Arthur Hsu, Sherman Hong, Luck Wing, Blanche Yee, Bill Yee, Raymond Wong, Randy Kwan, Richard Long, Jefferson Davis Hong, Leslie Bow, Sue Mae Bow, Doris Lee, Cedric Chinn, and James Wing.

I received genuine and gracious "Southern hospitality" during a visit to the Delta that allowed me to tour several towns, visit a few of the remaining stores, and talk with merchants about the grocery store life. These experiences enhanced my understanding and appreciation of the arduous lives of Chinese grocery merchants and their families. Frieda Quon at Delta State University and Blanche Yee, President of the Mississippi Lodge of the Chinese American Citizen's Alliance, were prime movers in arranging the visit and several opportunities to speak about my experiences growing up in Georgia during the 1940s.

I am again indebted to Professor Emeritus Judy Yung for her gracious response in giving time and expertise to offer invaluable suggestions that improved my focus. Special thanks go to Mel Brown for his generous advice, support, and good cheer. I was fortunate to have encouragement from other historians such as Sylvia Sun Minnick, Daniel Bronstein, Greg Robinson, Irwin Tang, and John Thornell.

November. 2008
Cypress, Ca.   JJ

Chopsticks in the Land of Cotton

Lives of Mississippi Delta Chinese Grocers

1. Why Chinese Came To The Delta

In the late 1860s and early 1870s, a small number of Chinese men, immigrants from the southeastern province of Guangdong, China, appeared for the first time in the Mississippi River Delta, a fertile land well suited for farming and prized for its rich source of cotton.

Where is the Delta?

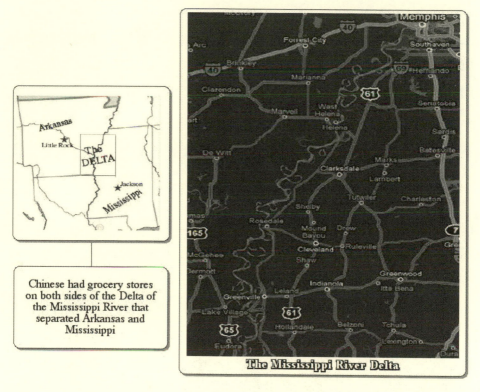

Figure 1 Location of the Mississippi River Delta with detailed view on right.

The Mississippi River serves as a major part of the boundary separating the states of Mississippi and Arkansas, as Figure 1 shows. On the Mississippi side of the river, the delta extends over 150 miles from north to south from just below Memphis southward to just above

Vicksburg and about 70 miles from Greenwood on the east to Greenville on the west encompassing these counties: Bolivar, Coahoma, Leflore, Humphreys, Issaquena, Quitman, Sharkey, Sunflower, Tunica, and Washington. The major cities and towns include Clarksdale, Cleveland, Greenville, Greenwood, Indianola, and Ruleville.

On the less populated Arkansas side of the river, there was also a rich agricultural region well suited for cotton, soybean, and wheat farming but fewer towns. In 1870 almost all of 98 Chinese there worked as farm laborers in Arkansas County, and by 1880, most of 133 Chinese lived in Jefferson and Chicot counties in small towns like Round Pond, Altheimer, Cotton Plant, Lake Village, and Hughes, with many working as sharecroppers on cotton plantations.[1]

Most of the Chinese grocers lived in the larger Mississippi Delta towns such as Clarksdale, Cleveland, and Greenville. Other Chinese grocers settled in small towns, most with between 500 to 1,000 inhabitants such as Sunflower, Louise, and Boyle.

All Delta towns were heavily populated with blacks, mostly cotton field workers. Over 90 percent of blacks in the United States in 1900 lived in the Deep South. Some towns like Cleveland and Greenville had as many as 70 percent black residents, and the lowest figures were around 40 percent in Clarksdale and Boyle. In the 1940s, there were 293,000 blacks in the Delta, which was three times more than the 98,000 whites. The presence of only about 500 Chinese was barely noticeable in most communities where they lived throughout the Delta among blacks and whites that together numbered almost 400,000.

---

[1] Lucy M. Cohen. *Chinese in the Post-Civil War South.* (Baton Rouge: Louisiana State University, 1984).

Since 1960, there has been a decline in the number of Chinese from Guangdong province, the source of the original immigrants, from an estimated peak of just above 1,200. The largest Chinese community, located in Greenville, may have lasted longer but eventually its Chinese population also shrank. Similarly, there has been a drop in the overall population of the economically impoverished Delta. For example, the total population also showed declines or little change in the 2000 census for the largest Mississippi communities such as Greenville, Clarksdale, and Cleveland, towns with populations ranging between 24,000 and 40,000.

Why Did Chinese Come to the Delta?

Why did they leave China, and what led them to come to the Delta? Unlike the thousands of other Chinese immigrants who settled in northern California seeking *gam sahn*, the fabled Gold Mountain, the Chinese entering the delta certainly were not enticed by prospects of wealth contained in any mountains of cotton, the dominant crop in the region for many years. The Chinese, never more than a few hundred until well after 1920, were a distinct minority in the Delta where the black cotton pickers were three or four times as numerous as whites.

The first Chinese immigrants from Guangdong Province started coming to the low-lying delta region bordering the Mississippi River around the middle of the 19th century. But long before the arrival of the first Chinese immigrants into this region, it was a white-dominated society. Prosperous white plantation owners purchased black slaves from Africa to perform the arduous labor of picking cotton by hand.

Figure 2 What shall we do with John Chinaman? (Artist unknown) Frank Leslie's Illustrated Newspaper, Sept. 25, 1869, 32.

However, with the abolition of slavery in 1863, white plantation owners no longer had their large supply of cheap labor and they searched desperately for replacements for the freed slave labor. The Chinese had already established a reputation as hard working and inexpensive workers on the farms in California and in railroad construction in the west.

Some labor suppliers had been successful in recruiting Chinese immigrant laborers to work at lower cost in other parts of the country. These successes in a Belleville, New Jersey laundry, a New England shoe factory, and a Pennsylvania cutlery factory prompted Southerners to seek a similar solution as shown in Figure 2. Leaders at a Memphis Convention of cotton planters in 1869 considered a proposal to have contractors hire Chinese laborers to replace blacks to punish them for acting like free men.

The cane field owners in Louisiana had already hired coolies who had been working in the West Indies and in Cuba.[2] Some Chinese laborers may have left the cane fields and drifted north into the Delta region where they found work on cotton plantations. Additional supplies of Chinese were recruited from China as well as from California to Arkansas and Mississippi to work in cotton fields in the 1870s. Another theory, undocumented or discredited, was that Chinese came on riverboats up the Mississippi to settle and soon open groceries in several Delta towns.[3]

The more plausible explanation is that several sources existed. Some Chinese in the Delta may have been men who had worked on railroad construction in the region. The Texas and the Yazoo Railroad in Mississippi had recruited Chinese to work on the railroads. Possibly some of them stayed and found work in the region after the railroad work ended. Another likely source were Chinese fleeing the violence and expulsion from parts of western United States to safer regions of the country.

Starting in the 1870s Chinese (as well as Italian) immigrants were recruited as farm laborers in the cotton fields of Van Buren, Lincoln, Jefferson and Pulaski and Arkansas counties, all located toward the center of the state, as part of a work force brought in by the Arkansas Valley Immigration Company. These men, mostly from California, were to work in the field for no more than five years for which they were paid the equivalent of several months of wages and provided with transportation

---

[2] Ibid.

[3] James W. Loewen, *The Mississippi Chinese: Between Black and White.* (Long Grove, Il.: Waveland Press, 1988).

to Arkansas. As many as 134 Chinese identified as farm laborers worked in Arkansas[4] while a smaller number appeared in the 1870 census schedules for Mississippi. However, about a year later, plantation owners discovered that the plan was not effective, as the Chinese did not do as well as blacks did in the fields.[5] In addition, disputes over nonpayment to Chinese workers arose that contributed to the Chinese deciding to open their own businesses.

Still, as late as 1880, bringing Chinese labor to the South continued as the New York Times reported that a Mississippi planter acknowledged that a Chinese labor contractor had been contacted and "…probably some Chinamen will be set to work in Southern Mississippi in a few weeks."[6]

There is no firm evidence about what happened to these men and whether they had descendants who stayed in the Mississippi River delta areas of Arkansas and Mississippi. It is possible that some stayed while some left for other regions, but it also conceivable that all of them left, as none of their names show up a decade later in the 1880 census schedules.

Early Work of Delta Chinese

Regardless of where they came from or how they managed to arrive in the Delta, once there, how did they earn a living? Early U. S. Census schedules from 1880 to 1910 show that Chinese in Arkansas and Mississippi operated laundries before they started grocery stores.

---

[4] Ibid. 149-171. Counts of Chinese were difficult as Chinese from Cuba and the West Indies often had Spanish surnames. Those with a Chinese and a non-Chinese parent were not counted as Chinese. Some blacks were counted as Chinese because the census recorded all Chinese as "Colored." Most of the Chinese listed in the 1870 Arkansas census were not born in China nor had Chinese surnames.
[5] Ibid.,
[6] "Chinese for the South." *New York Times*, March 9, 1880, 1.

However, by the 1920 census, the grocery store had essentially become the sole occupation of the Delta Chinese. It makes sense that laundry work would not have been in high demand in this mainly rural area. Perhaps some laundry men, once having saved a small amount from doing laundry, may have decided it would be more profitable to open grocery stores.

The opportunity for Chinese to open grocery stores expanded with the closure of plantation-owned and operated commissaries (See Figures 3 and 4) with the increasingly mechanized cotton production around the 1920s, which greatly reduced the need for manual labor. Until then, the plantation commissaries had been the main, if not the only source of food, clothing, and farming supplies to slaves, and eventually, sharecroppers who toiled in the cotton fields.

Figure 3 The commissary on the Sunflower, Ms. Plantation where cotton workers obtained food and supplies.

Figure 4 Cotton pickers shop at Marcella Plantation Commissary, Mileston, Ms., 1939. Library of Congress LC-USF34- 052200-D

White-owned grocery stores in the main business sections of town did not particularly welcome black customers.   The Chinese recognized the opportunity to carve an economic niche for themselves in Delta towns by filling this void.   Partnerships formed among male relatives help create a pool of shared capital called a *hui* that they could each, in turn draw from to allow them to open grocery stores typically located in black neighborhoods, providing convenience access for their primary sources of customers.

Furthermore, by extending credit to black workers until they were paid they gained an advantage over white stores, which had cash and carry policies. It was by no means an easy existence but it did afford them the opportunity to achieve some competitive advantage over white-owned stores.

White Supremacy in the Mississippi Delta

One cannot fully comprehend how difficult the lives of the Chinese in the Delta were without an understanding of the social dynamics of black-white interactions in the region. Segregation pitted whites and blacks in a one-sided adversarial relationship in which white rules governed social conduct. Whites had preference and privilege. Whites and blacks could not co-mingle in public settings wherever people sat down as in restaurants, theatres, or schools.

Despite the abolition of slavery by Lincoln, whites still held social, economic, and political power over blacks for well beyond the middle of the next century. Most townships in the Delta region had a higher percentage of blacks than whites, but the whites controlled the way of life in the highly segregated South. Whites instituted Jim Crow laws and traditions to preserve this way of life that favored whites. Segregation of blacks and whites was staunchly enforced. Blacks and whites had separate public drinking fountains and public toilet facilities. Blacks were required to ride in the back of transit buses and in separate cars on trains. Intimidation rather than enforcement was usually sufficient to have blacks comply with these social rules.

As cafes, restaurants, barbershops, schools, and churches for whites did not admit blacks, they had to start their own businesses, schools, and churches. There were separate picture show (movie) theatres for blacks and whites but some white theaters admitted blacks by creating separate seating sections for them (See Figure 5).

Figure 5 Entrance of Colored section balcony of a picture show theater, Belzoni, Ms., 1939. Library of Congress FSA/OWI COLL - E 915.

There were few work opportunities for blacks in the region and they mainly worked from dawn to dusk in the cotton fields of the delta plantations owned by whites. They lived in segregated neighborhoods in small substandard houses often in poorer condition than the one pictured in Figure 6.

Figure 6 Typical example of sharecropper housing. Library of Congress LC-USF33- 030570-M3.

Ecology of A Delta Town

What was the physical and social nature of the Delta towns in which the Chinese lived during the 1930s and 1940s when their grocery businesses flourished? A generalized image comes from detailed descriptions of one town by a Yale University psychology professor, John Dollard. He came to live in Indianola in Sunflower County for a few months in the late 1930s to observe racial interactions in the Delta. In his book he disguised its identity by referring to the town as "Southern town" rather than using its real name. Published in 1937 originally, *Caste and Class in a Southern Town*[7] became an influential ethnographic account of daily life interactions between blacks and whites in a segregated community.

Dollard gave the following description of the community life and daily routines in a typical small delta town.

> Four fifths of the land of the county is tilled, most of it undoubtedly in cotton. The town has a slight excess of females over males, and of Negroes over whites. Apparently, too, it includes most of the foreign-born of the county. These, observation indicates, are probably mainly Italians and Jews, with a very few Chinese. The median size of both white and Negro families is smaller in the town than in the county, but the white family remains about a full person larger than the Negro. Slightly more than 90 percent of the houses are one-family dwellings, and one cannot be sure that those with two or more families are not the overcrowded Negro cabins.
> .... it is probably an average small town in a rural county devoted to a staple crop and characterized by a black belt history and psychology. We know that 70.2 percent of the southeastern region is rural and that of the 29.8 percent of

[7] John Dollard. *Caste and class in southern town.* 2nd ed. (Garden City: Doubleday, 1949).

the population classed as urban, 15.2 percent lies outside of the metropolitan districts. It is in this latter group that our town falls. In type of economy it is certainly not typical of the whole south or even perhaps of the statistical mode in the southeastern region. It is rather more likely to represent an extreme of a general tendency, in some degree a relic of a by gone plantation and black belt culture. Attitudes here would certainly be different from those in towns and counties with smaller percentages of Negroes. They would likewise differ somewhat from social attitudes in metropolitan centers (Dollard, 1949, p.14-15).

Residential Segregation:

In the racially segregated communities of the Deep South, blacks and whites had their own well-defined residential and business neighborhoods outside the central business district.[8]

> The small industrial section devoted to ginning cotton and pressing cottonseed is isolated at one end of the town more or less in the Negro quarter. A square block of buildings and the four streets around it make up the business district. One street has six or seven department stores, owned and run almost exclusively by Jews. The thirsty traveler may stop and honk before one of the three drugstores and receive courteous curb service, although the polite northerner is frequently a little abashed at delivering a vulgar toot to a southern white man. He gets used to it, however, and is glad to feel the cool shock of a "coke" in the throat while still sitting in his automobile. There is a small and very hot hotel with an adjoining restaurant... One of the streets is lined with stores serving Negroes, though very few are owned by Negroes. A single floor of one building is reserved for the few Negro professional persons in the town...

---

[8]Dollard was criticized for misunderstanding the historical context of the Delta, poor sampling, and ignoring social class. His work fostered stereotypes that all whites were rich racists and all blacks were poor sharecroppers. Jane Adams & D. Gorton. "Southern trauma: Revisiting caste and class in the Mississippi Delta."*American Anthropologist, 106*, 2 (2004): 334-345.

Downtown of an evening, one of the streets is densely lined with cars. The center of this activity is the movie theater, white downstairs and colored in the gallery, with separate entrances. People are great moviegoers and discussers in this town. "Bank Night" in particular is memorable with the excitement of the drawing and a very bad picture to identify it. On Saturday the movie is invariably a Western picture, for then, we are told, the rural people come to town and they like "Westerns."

Saturday is by all odds the big day of the week. In the summer the stores are open all afternoon and evening (though closed on Thursday afternoons). The country Negroes mill through the streets and talk excitedly, buying, and enjoying the stimulation of the town crowds. The country whites are paler and less vivacious; there are not so many of them, but still a considerable number. "Rednecks," they are called, and their necks, it is true, are red, due to open shirts and daily exposure to the sun... Sunday is a quiet day on the white side. Through open church windows one hears organ and choir music. The Negroes take Sunday solemnly, too, but there seems a little more activity on their side of the town. (Dollard, 1949, pp. 4-5)

Downtown Clarksdale, 1941

Downtown Clarksdale in 1941 (See Figure 7) retained distinct areas from the past that separated people by race as well as social class, barriers that continued for many years.

The black, or Negro as it was called then, business district, consisted of a few square blocks centered on the corner of Fourth and Issaquena. All the black-owned businesses in Clarksdale, as well as those owned by a few Jewish, Italian, and Chinese families were located in this section. Clarksdale had a few immigrants, not always welcome by either blacks or whites, consisting of "about twenty-five or thirty families of Jewish storekeepers . . . a

few Greeks . . . a few Syrian families . . . and a few
Chinamen engaged in laundries . . . and some dope on the
side."[9]

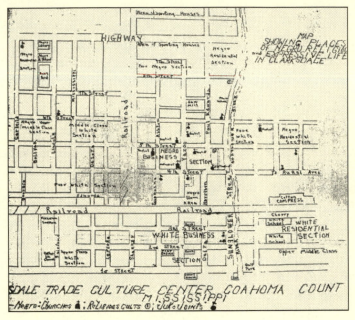

Figure 7 Map of white and black business and residential sections, Clarksdale, Ms., 1941.
Notice the social class distinction between residential areas for upper middle, middle class, and poor
for whites and Negro vs. poor Negro for blacks.[10]

Another observer noted:

> This part of town contained Clarksdale's only black hotel, the
> Savoy theater, a single furniture store, three gas stations, a
> host of jukes and cafés and beer parlors, barbershops, beauty
> parlors, groceries, and a funeral parlor. The two largest black
> churches stood directly across the street from the Dipsy
> Doodle, a favorite hangout for plantation blacks in the '30s

---

[9] Ibid. Adams' source for the immigrant breakdown was Abe Isaacson, who moved to
Clarksdale in 1914, quoted in History of Clarksdale and Coahoma County, (n.d.) 109.
However, there is no good evidence that Chinese laundries existed in Clarksdale after
1910.

[10] Samuel C Adams. *Changing Negro life in the Delta* (Nashville, TN: Fisk University, 1947).

who came to town on Saturday nights to dance, eat tamales, drink beer, and listen to the blues on the juke's Seabird, as they called the bright new Seeburg jukebox that sat in the middle of the floor.[11]

As in other Delta communities, both the race and social class of individuals determined where people lived in Clarksdale.

"Upper-middle-class whites lived on the other side of town, across the Sunflower River, whose bridge provided a direct route to the downtown shopping area with its banks, post office, and library. Black working class and day laborers lived in the Roundyard, a neighborhood just off the Negro business district that centered on a small area separated from white downtown by the railroad tracks that ran through the center of Clarksdale. The middle class of the Brickyard did not normally approve of the Roundyard's ways."[12]

Figure 8 Black cotton pickers selling to buyer, Belzoni, Ms. Library of Congress LC-USF33-030660-M4.

Figure 8 shows black cotton pickers congregating as they waited to sell their cotton to a buyer on a Saturday in Belzoni in the Negro section

---

[11] Quoted in Samuel C. Adams, *Changing Negro life.*

[12] Peter Rutkoff and Will Scott. "Preaching the Blues: The Mississippi Delta of Muddy Waters." *Kenyon Review*, Spring, 2005.

of town. This scene was similar to gatherings in other cotton towns like Clarksdale, Lexington, Greenville, or Cleveland.

How The Chinese Fit in A Black-White Society

One imagines that without such an imbalance of power in favor of whites over blacks, the lives of the Chinese immigrants to the region would have taken a quite different direction. Chinese, being neither black nor white, presented a problem for both blacks and whites in determining who they were. White supremacists simply felt if you are not white, then you are "Colored" irrespective of your culture, language, or origin. Although Chinese occupied a low social status, they were not mistreated as badly as blacks were in the Delta.

If Chinese had been successful laboring in the cotton fields, it would have been easier for both blacks and whites to consider them as "colored people," but of a lighter shade. However, the Chinese seized the opportunity to redefine their place in Delta society shortly after their arrival by establishing their presence as businessmen in small grocery stores. No longer farm laborers, they were merchants in a business that initially served primarily black workers.

Chinese were no longer so easily classified as "colored" because their role in society became more complicated. They were intermediaries or middlemen situated somewhere between black and white. Oddly, it was precisely because they were neither black nor white that the Chinese were able to work effectively with blacks and whites, groups that were rigidly separated by a long history of racial segregation throughout the South. The Chinese proved to be the "perfect grocer" for the pre-Civil rights era Delta society, as white merchants did not want to serve blacks.

Blacks themselves lacked monetary resources and cultural experiences to become merchants. Thus, the racial divide in the Delta created a vacuum that provided a viable economic niche for the Chinese that neither blacks nor whites could readily assume in this segregated society.[13]

However, the status of the Chinese grocers did vary somewhat in different towns, depending on whether most of their customers were white or black. When most customers were white, as was the case for stores located in the main business section of town, Chinese tended to be viewed as "inscrutable Orientals with wisdom Caucasians lacked." But where the stores were located in black neighborhoods and served mainly black customers, whites avoided their stores and viewed the Chinese with contempt.[14]

A leading white literary figure in the region, William Alexander Percy, in noting the abundance of Chinese storekeepers in the Delta, scornfully dismissed any contributions their presence made to the community:

> They are not numerous enough to present a problem
> __except to   the small white store-keeper__ but in so far as
> what wisdom they may inherit from Lao-Tse or Confucius
> they fail to impart.[15]

Chinese had more autonomy over their own economic fate than blacks did but they lacked the social power and influence that whites held.

---

[13] Mary Jo Schnieder and William M. Schneider "A structural analysis of the Chinese grocery store in the Missisippi Delta." In G. Sabo III and W. M. Schneider (Eds.) *Visions and Revisions: Ethnohistoric Perspectives on Southern Culture* (Athens, GA.: University of Georgia Press, 1987), 83-97.

[14] Ibid. 92.

[15] William Alexander Percy. *Lanterns on the Levee: Recollections of a Planter's Son.*. (Alfred A. Knopf, New York 1941), 18.

They had to rely on their predominantly black customer base to earn their living at the same time they were seeking better acceptance and fairer treatment from white society. To survive, Chinese had to establish good relations with blacks as well as whites, as both groups far exceeded them in numbers.

2. Lives of Early Delta Chinese Immigrants

The earliest U. S. census record showing Chinese in Mississippi was the 1870 schedule, which listed 16 Chinese male immigrants, all of whom were farm laborers working in Bolivar County. The entire state of Mississippi had only 129 Chinese, almost all men, listed in the 1880 U. S. census schedule. Three Chinese were operators of a restaurant in Leflore. In Ruleville, all the Chinese listed in that year were farm laborers. There were over 30 Chinese listed in the 1880 census living in Greenville and at least two, Heng King and Sing Long, had opened grocery stores. One couple, Charley and Mary Fung, ran a laundry. By 1900 in Greenville there were as many as 7 laundrymen working at 229 Walnut Street. However, unlike in most parts of the country, few Chinese engaged in the laundry business.

Mississippi had the largest number of Chinese immigrants in the South in 1910, with 174, and in 1920 with 211, mainly in Washington County (Greenville), Coahoma County (Clarksdale), and Bolivar County (Cleveland).

The highest census count for Chinese in Arkansas was in 1880, at a meager number of 125. But the count dropped to as low as 43 by 1910, before rising to 55 in 1920. Only a small percentage, however, were actually in the Delta region of the state. Much larger numbers of Italian laborers were recruited but they were more widely distributed across the state rather than concentrated in the Delta. Greenville, had the most Chinese in 1900, 60, but by 1920 it was down to 22 while the number in Bolivar County doubled from 25 to 52 over the same 20 years, according to the census. Other towns like Rosedale, Cleveland, Clarksdale, Duncan, Pace, Merigold, Drew, and Alligator had only a handful of Chinese. The majority of these small towns had no more than 1 or 2 Chinese families.

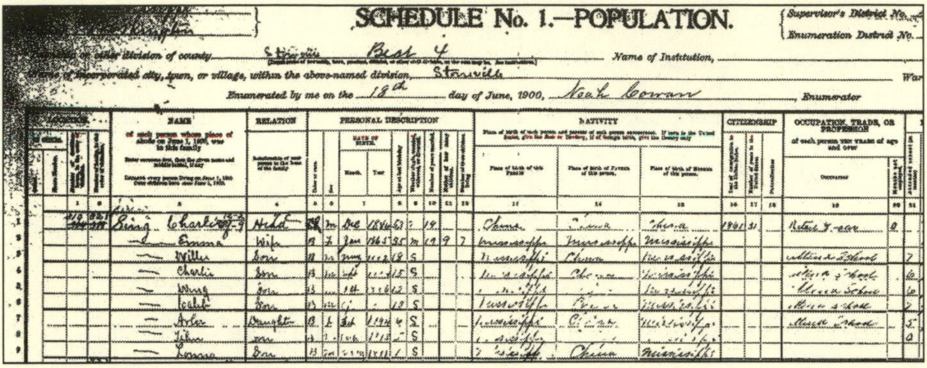
SCHEDULE No. 1.—POPULATION.

Supervisor's District No.

Enumeration District No.

Name of Institution,

Enumerated by me on the 18th day of June, 1900, Noah Cowan, Enumerator

Figure 9 1900 U. S. Census schedule listing Charley Sing and Emma Clay and their 5 children in Stoneville, Washington County, retail store.

Oral histories confirm the view that as early as the 1870s some Chinese who had worked on railroads did settle briefly in Stoneville near Greenville and may have engaged for a while in farm work. One of the earliest to arrive in 1861 was Wong On, identified in the 1900 U. S. Census as Charley Sing. Around the 1870s, he may have been the first Chinese to open a small grocery store to serve sharecroppers.

Chinese recruited originally for farm labor, however, soon rejected or abandoned it to seek other forms of work. Cotton picking was backbreaking labor that lasted from sunrise to sunset in the humid and scorching heat of Mississippi summers. Some Chinese probably left the region, but others remained and before long discovered they could earn a living by opening small grocery stores in towns all over the Delta.

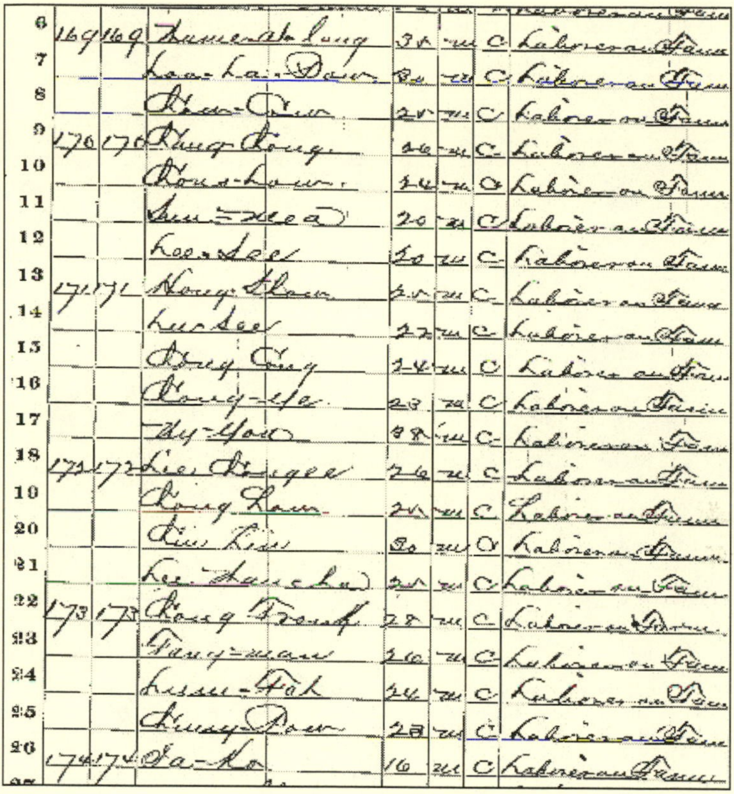

Figure 10 Chinese farm laborers, 1870 U. S. Census Schedule. Silver Lake, Arkansas County, Arkansas.

With the failed experiment using Chinese for farm labor, white cotton planters had to rely entirely on black sharecroppers to pick the cotton from the fields. Sharecropping was a system when the landowner would lease land to the tenant, provide minimal housing, some provisions, farm implements, and a 'furnish' of cash for minimal living expenses. At the end of the season, the owner deducted these advance payments from the profits, if any, obtained from the sharecropper's yield. A sharecropper then had to split what was left with the landowner so he barely made ends meet, as the financial arrangements dictated by the plantation owners were always to their advantage. The system was a feudal one in which the landowner was the lord, and the workers were his lowly vassals.

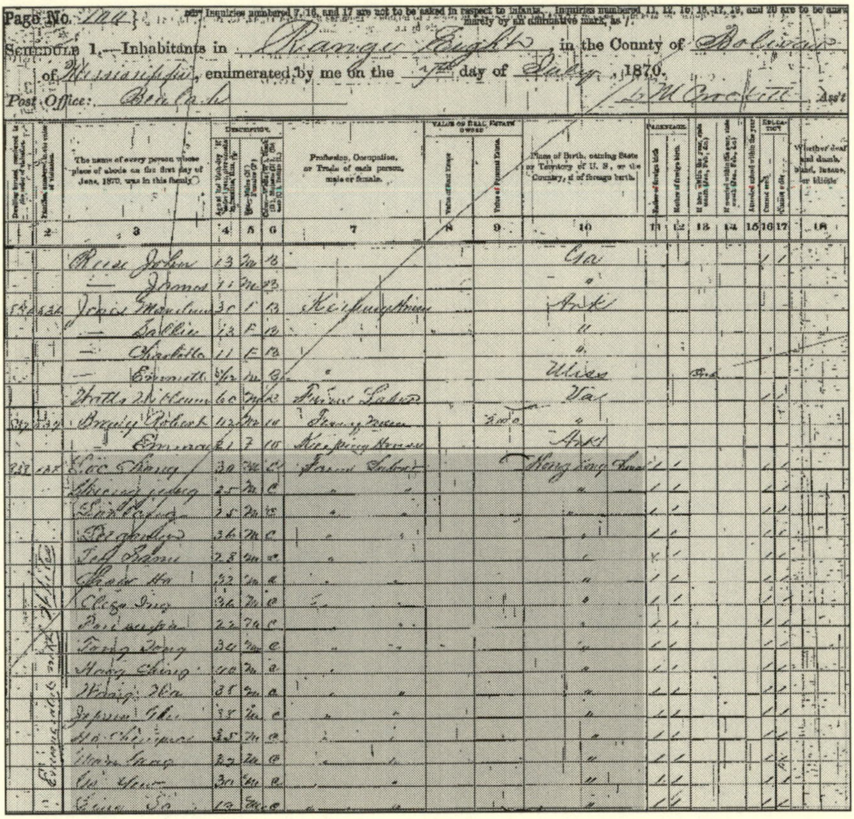
Page No. 100 } Inquiries numbered 7, 16, and 17 are not to be asked in respect to infants. Inquiries numbered 11, 12, 15, 16, 17, 18, and 20 are to be answered merely by an affirmative mark, as /.

Schedule 1.—Inhabitants in Range Eight, in the County of Bolivar, of Mississippi, enumerated by me on the 17th day of July, 1870.

Post Office: Beulah

Figure 11 U. S. Census Schedule listing of 16 Chinese farm laborers (shaded) at Beulah, Ms, Bolivar County, 1870.

As a northern journalist described the land and the labor of its sharecropper inhabitants in a newspaper article:

> Black of the rich earth and green of the springing cotton plants stretch from horizon to horizon. This is the fabulous Mississippi Delta, last outpost of feudalism in America. Here is land more fertile than any other in the world. Here close to half a million Negroes toil from childhood to the grave in the service of King Cotton, from sunup to sundown if they share-crop, from 6 to 6 if they work by the day.

Here are feudal baronies that run from 5,000 to 20,000 acres, where as many as 6,000 sharecropper families, wives and children, parents and grandparents follow the one mule plow and the chopping hoe all their lives. On these tight little Delta principalities "The Man" (the landlord) is the middle justice, the high and the low. Mississippi law stops dead in its tracks at their boundaries. No sheriff, no peace officer takes a man, black or white off these acres until "The Man" tells him he may.[16]

Expansion of Chinese Grocery Stores

The U. S. Census showed that some Chinese living in Washington County operated grocery stores as early as 1880. By 1900, Issaquena had six Chinese running one store as well as another three Chinese partners operating another grocery. In 1910 Greenville had as many as 10 grocers, some operated by U.S.- born Chinese who came to the Delta from California and Louisiana. There was a grocery and a laundry run by Chinese in Rosedale, Bolivar County, in 1910. Another laundry existed in Clarksdale.

By 1920, there were 208 Chinese in the entire state, but only six of them were adult women. The census listed only two girls, a 10-year old and a 1-year old, both with a China-born father but an American-born mother of unspecified race.

A somewhat curious aspect of census records is that the Chinese listed in three counties (Coahoma, Bolivar, and Washington) in one decade were an almost entirely different set of individuals from those listed there only a decade earlier. Such divergences occurred for comparisons of 1900 with 1910, and for 1910 with 1920. These changes

---

[16] Ray Sprigle. "Feudalism Lives on In the Delta." *Pittsburgh Post-Gazette,* Aug. 24, 1948, 1.

would make more sense for the 1870 or 1880 census when many Chinese were laborers.[17] But for the 1900 and later census, when most Chinese were merchants, not laborers, this shift is surprising.

One possible explanation is that some Chinese moved from one town to another every few years in search of better earnings or that they moved to join relatives in their stores. On the other hand, changes in census listings may simply reflect the fact that older Chinese may have died or returned to China between censuses. Also, some middle-aged Chinese may have been temporarily in China for visits with their wives and families in China. Any or all of these factors could have contributed to the total turnover in census listings of Chinese recorded only a decade apart.

Increased Migration to the Delta in Late 1800s

After the initial Chinese grocery stores opened and began to succeed, some Chinese convinced some of their kin in other parts of the country to join them in the Delta. As already noted, Chinese were not welcome in many western states and received real or threatened violence. Many were anxious to move to regions where there were fewer Chinese in hopes they would be better treated. They came to the Delta from places as far away as California and New York for this reason.

In addition, successful merchants had their brothers, uncles, cousins, and sons come from China to help in the business. Many of the Chinese in the Delta came from the same villages in Guangdong and had the same or similar surnames such as Jue and Joe (also spelled Chow, depending on the pronunciation).

---

[17] No analysis was possible for 1890 because a fire destroyed those records.

The large supply of inexpensive Chinese labor throughout the nation was blamed for an economic depression in the United States that started in the 1870s and lasted until near the end of the century. The increased hostility toward them led to the passage of the Chinese Exclusion Act in 1882. This law was the only one ever passed that singled out a single race from immigrating to the U. S. It prohibited Chinese laborers such as farm workers from coming, and it also prevented laborers already here from bringing wives and children in China join them in the U. S.

The Chinese Exclusion Act presented a major obstacle to Chinese immigration as severe restrictions were imposed on which Chinese could gain entry. Laborers were categorically denied entry while merchants could enter with proof of their status. In addition, they could bring in family members but had to provide extensive proof of kinship.

For example, when the earlier mentioned Charley Wong, a grocer in Yazoo City, wanted to make a return visit to China in 1909, he was required to produce two witnesses. They had to testify that Wong was a merchant by declaring that they had never seen him engaged in manual labor as shown in Figure 12.[18] Moreover, witnesses had to be white, if their declarations were to be readily accepted by immigration officers. Given how isolated most Chinese were in the Delta, finding two white witnesses was not a simple accomplishment.

[18] Transcript of Interrogation of Charley Wong. Immigration Service, Malone, New York. File 6400/537 33/64 Box 223, Oct. 2, 1909.

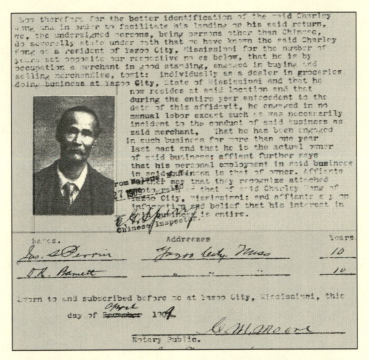

Figure 12 Affidavit Charley Wong had to file before a return visit to China in 1909 to document his merchant status for his return. Immigration File 6400/537 33/64.

A Bachelor Society

The exclusion law had a major adverse impact on Chinese communities throughout the U. S., creating bachelor societies inhabited mostly by single men or married men separated for years from their wives and children who were still in their Guangdong villages.

Chinese laborers that came to the Delta starting around the 1870s were typically young single men. After earning enough money, they would go back to China and marry through matches arranged for them, as was the custom then. After remaining for up to one year or two in China, and in some cases, having children, they would leave their wives to return to their work in the U. S. Some might return every few years and sire additional children before returning to the U. S. to work, sending remittances to support their families from their saved earnings. Some men hoped to return to China and saw no need to bring their families to the U. S. Others eventually managed to save enough to bring their families over.

Some Chinese men, even if they had wives in China, had conjugal relationships with Black women. Exactly how many Chinese men engaged in sexual relationships with black women is hard to determine, as they were kept secret, whenever possible. Such arrangements were hardly surprising given that there were very few Chinese women in the region for several decades and return visits to China were infrequent and for short durations. However, Chinese men entering such relationships invoked strong ostracism. Mixed race sexual relationships, even in marriage, were not generally accepted. Chinese, blacks, and whites all had minimal contact with mixed race couples and children from such unions suffered rejection as well.

Not much is known about how the couple in the Chinese-black marriage, Wing On and Emma Clay, mentioned at the start of this chapter dealt with social rejection. They had a large family, with 13 children, and these mixed race children had a lonely existence. They were shunned by black, as well as by white children, according to accounts given by the oldest daughter, Arlee. Not allowed to attend white schools, they received poorer education from the under funded black schools. Arlee had a close relationship with her father and developed a Chinese identity.[19] She married a Chinese grocer, J. S. Hen in Greenville where most other

---

[19] Ruthanne Lum McCunn (1988). "Arlee Hen and Black Chinese" In *Chinese American Portraits: Personal Histories 1828-1988*. San Francisco: Chronicle Books, 79-87.

Chinese had a low regard for them.[20] Her sister, El-Dee Sing also married a Chinese grocer in Greenville, Fung Goon Lee.[21] Other Chinese in the Delta had sexual relationships with local non-Chinese women, mainly black, and in some cases, had children from these liaisons. For example, Charley Wong was married for 18 years and had four children with a non-Chinese wife.

Another Chinese who married a black woman, Joe Chow aka Joe Bing, came from Guangdong to San Francisco in the early 1920s as a student. After finishing his education, he worked for a Chinese family. After he earned enough money, he learned of opportunities for work in the grocery business in Cleveland, Mississippi. Sometime in the late 1920s, he eventually opened a grocery store there. Relatives believe that he had a wife and son in China that he left behind when he came to the U. S. In any event, in 1933 he married a black woman, Hazel Taylor from Cleveland, in probably a common law arrangement. They had four sons, Joe, Jr., Kenneth, Edward, and Charles but life in the Delta for a mixed race family was often made difficult by the racial attitudes of the time.

> Because they were an interracial couple, police harassed them periodically. Around the end of 1935, Joe opened a second grocery store that his wife managed at 200 Eureka Street in Greenville, a more tolerant town. Joe spent the weekdays running the Cleveland store and on weekends was at the Greenville store with Hazel and their children. In 1938, the store suffered a fire of suspicious origin but there was no proof that it was racially motivated. Around 1942, Joe decided to close both stores and move to Houston, Texas.

---

[20] Arlee Hen, Interview with Judy Yung at Greenville, Mississippi, December 1982. *Chinese Women of America Research Project*, Chinese Culture Foundation of San Francisco.
[21] Christopher Lee, e-mail to Author, Sept. 24, 2008.

However, soon afterwards, the marriage did not survive. [22]

Chinese rejected Black-Chinese marriages, and the children from them, for several reasons. A major concern was that whites would treat Chinese as badly as they did blacks if they intermarried with blacks. Additionally, some Chinese had prejudices themselves against blacks.

Bringing Wives and Families From China

The immigration law classified Chinese grocers as merchants rather than laborers, which was highly favorable for them. The exclusion law allowed merchants to bring wives and children over from China, but denied this possibility for those laborers already here. From 1903 to 1923, over half of the Chinese immigrants (33 of 60) to the Delta held merchant status and another 13 were, or claimed to, be their sons from China. Unlike the case in most other regions of the country, none were laborers.[23]

There were very few Chinese women in the Delta but their numbers slowly increased over the 1920s. In addition, some Delta grocers married American-born Chinese women through mostly arranged marriages from other sections of the U. S. Finally, Chinese in the Delta began to enjoy family life as evidenced by census records showing the birth of 11 Chinese children in the Delta by 1923.[24]

Paper Sons

In response to the grossly unfair exclusion law, Chinese developed

---

[22] Kristin Chow e-mail to Author, Aug. 5, 2008. August 14, 2008
[23] Personal communication, March 1, 2008. Daniel Bronstein tabulation of immigration files.
[24] Ibid.

ways to circumvent immigration restrictions. Some merchants routinely filed false reports of the birth of a son to immigration authorities each time they returned from visits to China. These claims created 'slots' for future immigration of fictitious sons because they could be sold to young men who were not their sons seeking to come to the U. S. Sometimes, men returned to China upon retirement and sold their identity papers to younger men.

These "paper sons," as they came to be known as, had to assume the name on the immigration documents. In all instances, the fictive son had to memorize many details about the family and village of the person whose identity he was assuming because immigration officials interrogated them extensively as they tried determine the authenticity of their claimed relationship. It was a grueling experience as those applicants that could not answer the barrage of questions satisfactorily could be deported.

One consequence of the bachelor society was the limited family life among the Chinese in the region even as late as 1920. By then, over a dozen men were listed as working in grocery stores but the only clear evidence of any Chinese family was a census listing showing that a Chinese man, head of a merchant store in Leland, and a Mississippi-born woman of unstated race lived with a 17-year old girl, Bessie Woo.

However, by the 1930 U. S. census an increase in the numbers of Chinese grocers with families occurred. Chu Ting and his wife Dird Shee operated a grocery store at 640 Theobold Street in Greenville with their three children, Joseph, Ying, and Margaret. Rosedale had at least 2 grocers, both with families in 1930. Lee Chon operated a retail grocer store in Sunflower with his wife Willie and two daughters, Dorothy and

Mildred. In Tunica, Quay Wing, and his wife Suit Shee, owned a general store. They had several Mississippi born children, Joe Ping, Jimet Pang and Mary Pang. Although Chinese opened more grocery stores and began the creation of families by 1930, their numbers were still very small in comparison to the total population.

Chinese and the Ethnic Balance

The influx of Chinese into the region posed a problem for the relationship of whites to other groups, potentially changing the relationship among racial groups. At its twentieth century peak around 1960, the Chinese population in the Delta was only about 1,000 to 1,200, less than 5 percent of the total population. Chinese eventually gained in status and although they were not considered the equal of whites, whites viewed them more favorably than blacks.

Chinese stressed family values, and strong familial ties. When the first Chinese arrived, many of them did not have wives or families with them, having left them in China. But when possible, they recruited family members, brothers, sons, uncles, and cousins to come work with them. The family commitment helped Chinese became successful merchants because all family members worked cooperatively in the stores. Chinese valued education, and parents urged their children to do well in school.

How did they manage to fit in between the two opposing communities? Blacks benefited from having Chinese grocery stores in their neighborhoods and generally accepted their presence. They became well established and blended into the community. One black from the Mississippi Delta recalled encountering Chinese families while shopping with his grandmother in the small town of Itta Bena with this reflection:

It was whites, their power as individuals and as families, that commanded the attention of blacks in the Mississippi Delta then and now. The Chinese of the Delta were mysterious, inasmuch as they were largely an unknown quantity. Most blacks knew them only in the context of conducting business at the local grocery stores they owned. Little was known about their personal lifestyles. On reflection, it seems the Chinese were separate from whites; somehow different, not as powerful, not as dangerous and more respected by whites than blacks were. Beyond this vague image of the Chinese, blacks gave little thought to their presence in the black community.[25]

Chinese immigrants had some commonalities with another immigrant group, Italian farm laborers, who were far more numerous than Chinese in both Arkansas and Mississippi. They also faced prejudice from native white Southerners, even suffering a few instances of lynching. Italians were foreigners, and Catholics, who did not share the Southern values and traditions of white supremacy and Protestant faiths.

Eventually the Italians managed to start their own businesses as grocers, fruit peddlers, confectioners, and shoemakers. They, like the Chinese, were more accepting of blacks than were southern whites. Nonetheless, skin color was a strong factor underlying how people were treated. Being white, Italians as did Lebanese immigrants in the Delta, eventually achieved better treatment and social status than either Chinese or blacks managed.

---

[25] Ronald Love. Review of *Lotus Among the Magnolias: The Mississippi Chinese*, by Robert Seto Quan in collaboration with Julian B. Roebuck. *Social Forces, 62*, 3, (1984): 832-833.

Figure 13 Cotton hoers, Hopson Plantation cotton fields, Clarksdale Ms. Library of Congress LC-USF33- 030948-M2

In contrast, blacks were, for the most part, poorly paid laborers in the cotton fields. Many black families were fragmented as a consequence of slavery, and the absence of fathers in the home placed greater burdens on the mothers. Even in families where fathers were present, they often could not afford to support wives and children. Unable to build economic resources, blacks could not easily become entrepreneurs or open their own businesses, and had to depend on working as laborers or employees, subject to layoffs and low wages. Jim Crow laws and traditions, combined with poor educational opportunities, kept blacks at the bottom of the social ladder.

Chinese Groceries in black neighborhoods

Chinese grocery stores in these segregated communities were almost always located in black neighborhoods. For example, according to the 1920 census schedule, there were few Chinese in Clarksdale but one Chinese grocer, Joe Young, had a store at 540 Ashton St. In 1946 another Chinese market was located at 370 Yazoo St. All of these locations were described on the 1941 map of Clarksdale as a Negro business or slum area.

The 1920 census showed that the Chinese were expanding beyond grocery stores into cafes and restaurants. Two Chinese opened a restaurant at 340 Issaquena St. in the black business section and a second one existed, but its location was not identifiable from records.[26]

Sojourner Outlook

Most of the early Chinese in the Delta, as in other regions of the United States and Canada, came only to earn a living to help their impoverished families back in China. The initial plan did not involve establishing permanent residence in another country. Their goal was to make their fortune here and then return to China to be with their wives, children, and parents.

As Ed Joe recalled about his father's plans for the future:

> My dad has always before the war, the Second World War, said that we were going to make our living and go back to China. Well, we were raised in Mississippi, and we didn't want to go back to China… their (parents) main thing was to make their fortune and go back home. In their minds their family was over there.[27]

This sojourner outlook played an important role on their lives and contributed to their disinterest in becoming assimilated to American customs and values. The immigrants maintained their Chinese identity

---

[26] These early restaurants were run by Chinese but they were not "Chinese restaurants" in the current form, which serve Chinese cuisine; as elsewhere at the time they probably served mostly local dishes prepared in American style.

[27] Edward and Annette Joe. Interview by Kimberly Lancaster and Jennifer Mitchell, May 1, 2000 transcript. Delta State University Oral History Archives, Cleveland, Ms.

and ties to their homeland. However, the subsequent course of world events, especially the rise of Communist China in 1949 thwarted most Chinese immigrants from fulfilling this plan. Dreams of a return to China soon died, and the Chinese here as throughout the country began to realize that their futures lay in the United States.

3. Why Grocery Stores, And Not Laundries?

Some historical accounts state simply that Chinese brought to work in the cotton fields soon left this way of earning a living, preferring to open small grocery stores, similar to the inclinations of Chinese in other parts of the country to own other small businesses such as laundries and restaurants rather than work as employees.[28] However, none of these analyses provide much detail about how they managed to make this transition. Lacking much money, and probably with little English language proficiency, how likely was it that Chinese laborers could quickly make the transition to become grocery store operators? This is a question that has been largely unaddressed in earlier studies. In the case of one store, it seems that one Chinese was able to obtain a loan about $600 of merchandise from a Lebanese to establish his grocery store.[29] That might account for the origin of one store, but other mechanisms would be needed to explain how so many other grocers got started.

Chinese grocers throughout the Delta had to establish good relationships with wholesale food distributors. For instance, in the late 1920s wholesale grocers in Clarksdale and in Memphis (such as Malone and Hyde and Liberty Cash Groceries) were willing to sell to Chinese grocers by providing merchandise in advance of payment because they felt the Chinese were good merchants. Wholesalers would initially stock the store with all kinds of merchandise on credit. Each week they would replenish the stock for each store. At that time, the Chinese grocers

---

[28] James W. Loewen. *The Mississippi Chinese.*
[29] Sally Chow Interview by John Jung, Aug. 28, 2007.

would pay for their previous purchase and however much they could afford to pay down on the balance of what they owed for the initial inventory. The wholesalers did not demand any set amount nor have terms for payment, but in return they expected the Chinese to be regular customers.[30]

Another plausible explanation of how some Chinese obtained sufficient capital to purchase inventory for a grocery store is that they saved money from working in some other occupation first. By the 1870s Chinese throughout the United States had become laundrymen in large numbers.[31] Laundry work was initially uncontested by whites, although it did meet with resistance from black washerwomen in some areas. Laundry work did not require much capital or equipment other than a washboard, iron, water, and soap to begin in comparison to grocery stores, which required more capital to purchase merchandise to stock the store. Some Chinese, with saved earnings from running laundries, were in a position to make the move to grocery stores. Once successful, they urged relatives in other parts of the country, or in China, to come and join in operating the business.

Were There Chinese Laundries in the Delta?

There is evidence that Chinese operated laundries in towns on both sides of the river as early as 1870. In Greenville 28 year-old Charley Fung ran a laundry on Mulberry Street with his wife, Mary. Born in Louisiana, it is likely that she was black rather than Chinese since there were few Chinese women in the United States then (See Figure 14).

---

[30] Linn K. Pang, Comments, April 10, 2008.

[31] John Jung *Chinese Laundries: Tickets to Survival on Gold Mountain.* (Cypress, Ca.: Yin and Yang Press, 2007).

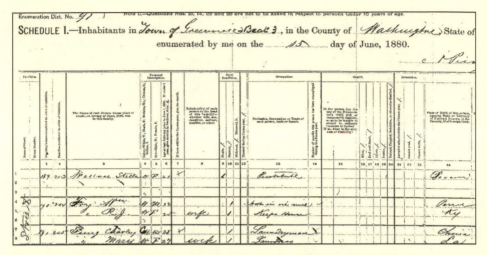

Figure 14 1880 Census Schedule listing of Greenville laundry of Charley and Mary Fung.

Charley Wong, mentioned earlier in Chapter 1, testified to immigration authorities that he had previously operated a laundry for eight years in Natchez, Mississippi before he entered the grocery business in Yazoo City. An immigration officer went to the business site to verify his testimony. Another example involved a grocer in Greenville who worked in a laundry in Paducah, Kentucky, when he first arrived from China.[32]

Operating a laundry may have been the entry point into self-employment for other Chinese as well. Census figures show that several laundries existed as early as 1870 in Madison, Clarksdale, and Greenville. Census records show about 5 to 10 Chinese on both the Arkansas and Mississippi sides of the river operated laundries between 1880 and 1910, but none of these men appear again in the subsequent census schedule for the same state a decade later.

[32]Luck Wing. Interview by Kimberly Lancaster, 1 March 2000.transcript, Delta State University Oral History Archives, Cleveland, Ms.

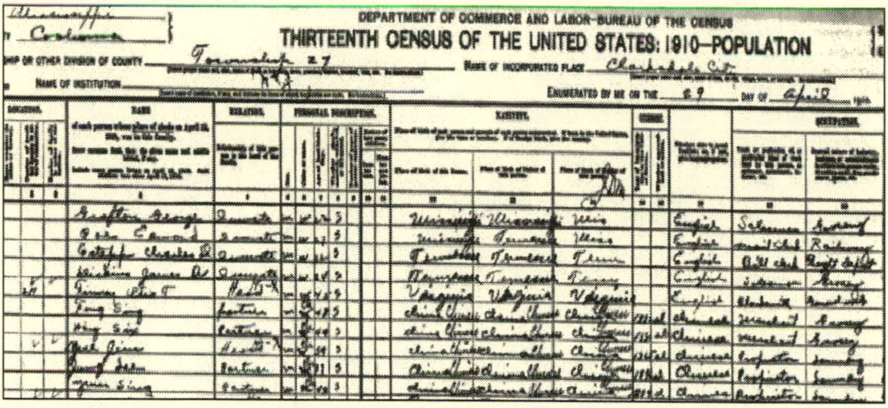
DEPARTMENT OF COMMERCE AND LABOR—BUREAU OF THE CENSUS

THIRTEENTH CENSUS OF THE UNITED STATES: 1910—POPULATION

Figure 15 Two grocery and 3 Chinese laundries in Clarksdale, 1910 U. S. Census Schedule.

The 1927 City Directory shows that Hop Lee had the only Chinese laundry in Greenville at 122 Walnut Street near the levee.[33] U. S. Census Schedules confirm its presence at that location as early as 1910 but it was quite possibly the last one in the Delta. Chinese laundries seem to have vanished from the region at about the same time that Chinese grocery stores started to proliferate. Some laundrymen may have moved to another state, returned to China, or died. But it is also possible that some switched to grocery stores in the Delta or in other states, which offered better opportunities for profit.

How or why did the Chinese switch from laundries to grocery stores? The demand for clean, starched, and ironed laundry was probably lower in the small Delta towns than it was in large cities such as Chicago and New York where laundries thrived for many years. Working in the fields picking cotton all day under a broiling sun did not require clean clothes, as would be the case for business men and office workers. For the poor

---

[33] I thank Hugh McCormick for locating this listing in the 1927 Greenville City Directory.

black cotton pickers, buying food was a higher priority than having freshly laundered clothing every day.

By the 1880s, Chinese opened grocery stores in Greenville and before long in other Delta communities like Cleveland, Greenwood, and Clarksdale on one side of the river and in towns like Holly Grove, Helena, Blytheville, Hughes, Cotton Plant, and Round Pond on the Arkansas side of the Delta.

Blacks often lacked enough money to pay cash for food supplies, which white merchants required. Chinese store owners were willing to extend credit to black customers, and let them have grocery items when they were needed and allow them to settle their account when they received their pay at the end of the week or month. Here is an example of how this system operated.

> ...say this week a customer charged $10. He paid the ten dollars next week when he came to the store, but he would then charge $15 of a new purchase. The week following, he paid the $15 and then charged $20 of purchase. He kept escalating the charges in this way till the charge reached about $50 -- then he would not show up for a long while or at all. When he did return, he usually paid only $10 toward the overdue balance, and started charging a new purchase.
> ... this practice of escalating charges and non-payment of debts created a lot of headaches and problems for the grocers. It was not worth the trouble and money to pursue collection of bad debts legally. Debt collection by legal means also would present an ugly image to the customers. The storeowners simply forfeited these long-overdue payments. In order to absorb the losses from uncollected debts, the grocers usually had to raise the prices of the groceries. Since there were no legally written agreements,

these uncollected debts could not be deducted from income taxes of the storeowners.[34]

Figure 16 Ray Joe was an influential Chinese community leader for the Delta Chinese in the 1930s and 1940s. He and his wife ran the Joe Yuen Company grocery store in Itta Bena, Ms.

Locating their stores in black neighborhoods was not entirely a deliberate choice or strategy of the Chinese. Segregation prevented them from living in white neighborhoods so they were forced to live in black areas. This barrier proved to be advantageous for many reasons. It was more convenient to live close to their primary customers, the blacks, and the store rent was lower than it would have been in the central business district. Additionally, by living in the backs of their stores, they also saved the expense of renting another space for living quarters. Since they worked long into the night, it was safer to sleep in their stores than to go home late at night and risk assault. Being on the premises 24 hours a day also enabled them to protect their merchandise from burglary.

Most of the early stores were small, as might be expected, but eventually many grocers expanded their inventory beyond basic food

---

[34] Zhou Liang, "Life of a Chinese American Grocer in the South," *China Daily*, 1961. Nd, Zhou Liang, Translation from Chinese to English, 2001.

items like milk, bread, and eggs. They became community general stores selling meat, produce, beer, wine, and whiskey as well as dry goods and hardware. Farm supplies such as feed and seed were another source of income. Salesmen from distributors came to the store weekly to take orders, which would be sold on credit and delivered to the store but peddlers also were a source of smaller quantities of food items.

> Our store was large so we had a wareroom for feed, hardware, etc. We were a general store. Otherwise inventories didn't have to be too big because of weekly shipments ... Sometimes my Dad had to go pick up meat or other products for the store ... sometimes peddlers came by with watermelons, syrup, pottery, etc. to sell ... salesmen would come buy weekly to take the orders in person and the delivery trucks would bring the goods ... mostly on credit and some COD. My Dad even used an abacus and later adding machines to keep books ...he used single-entry bookkeeping.[35]

In 1941, almost all of the 900 Chinese in the Mississippi Delta were related to merchants operating grocery stores. Of the 132 Chinese businesses in Arkansas in 1949, 125 were grocery stores as opposed to 1 laundry, 1 radio and watch repair shop, and 5 restaurants.[36] Around that time, Greenville had, by far, the highest number of Chinese grocery stores at 52, followed by Greenwood, 26, Clarksdale, 24, Vicksburg, 15, and Cleveland, 11. Other towns such as Hollandale, Shaw, and Moorhead each had 7 while Boyle, Itta Bena, and Tutwiler had each 6.[37]

> There are no Chinese hand laundries, curio shops, chop suey cafes, or lottery establishments. The Chinese has established

---

[35] Bobby Joe Moon e-mail message to Author, July 10, 2007

[36] Pao Yun Liao *A Case Study of a Chinese Immigrant Community.* Master's Thesis, Sociology, University of Chicago, 1951.

[37] *Tri-State Chinese Directory of Mississippi, Arkansas, and Tennessee.* Undated, Greenwood, Ms.: Chinese Commercial Directory Service Bureau.

himself in the role of the retail cash grocer and he is attempting to defend and expand that position. There may be poor white and Negro sharecroppers, but there are no Chinese in this economic class. Nearly all of the stores are operated by men, but there are notable exceptions; for example, the widow Ho-Shee, who has run a grocery store in for 14 years.[38]

Figure 17 Inside an early Chinese grocery store, location unknown. Courtesy, Delta State Archives, Cleveland, Ms.

Much of the success of Chinese grocery stores could be credited to the family, broadly defined, involvement. Many of these businesses were family enterprises that involved the labor of wives and children. Some stores included extended family members such as brothers, uncles, nephews, and cousins who often came from other parts of the country or from China.

---

[38] Robert W. O'Brien. "Status of Chinese in the Mississippi Delta." *Social Forces, 19*, 3, (1941): 386-390.

By having all immediate family members contribute time and effort, the grocer did not pay wages, as was the common practice for many small businesses such as laundries and restaurants operated by Chinese.[39] Family members received money for living expenses as well as meals and housing. Other relatives who worked in the store generally received free meals and housing behind or near the store.

Some relatives paid around $500 or $1000 to become partners, and eventually some were placed in charge of another store location if the business expanded. By having several stores, the grocer could obtain lower wholesale costs by purchasing larger quantities of merchandise, which might be stockpiled in a nearby warehouse.

Business records of sales, invoices, and payments, if kept at all, typically were not very thorough, and would likely not survive an external audit. Undoubtedly, some underreporting of sales and over-reporting of expenses occurred for income tax filings. This loose accounting helped improve "profits."

Chinese grocers soon earned the respect and admiration of many whites in their communities with their skill as businessmen, industriousness, and competitiveness. They were seen as good members of their community. White views of the Chinese merchants are reflected by the following answer of a white merchant in an interview.

> In regard to your question about the Chinese grocery stores here, I'd hate to be against them in the grocery business. They open up before anyone else, and stay open later and do more business than anybody else in town. They are really dedicated to their stores. When we first came here, the

---

[39] Alfred Yee. *Shopping at Giant Foods: Chinese Supermarkets in Northern California.* (Seattle: University of Washington Press, 2003).

Chinese were living in the back of their stores, and they opened at five in the morning and often didn't close until midnight, and there was always some member of the family in the store. They worked like a bunch of ants. There are several large supermarkets here, but they can't hold a candle to these Chinese. The prices in the Chinese stores are always good, and their profit margin is not all that high. But these Chinese are funny in a way . . .

You don't think of them as Chinese, but just as one of us. [Chinese Merchant] is president of the Chamber of Commerce and he does a good job. His brother used to be president, and he did a good job too. Sometimes I think that they do too much business with the Negroes, but everybody has to do something with them because there are so many of them here in ... The Chinese are respected and looked up to here because they do their job and mind their business. I've never known a Chinese to default on a note, or not to live up to their obligations right on the dot. They are honest with everybody.[40]

Blacks generally had high regard for Chinese grocers as good businessmen, although some had mixed feelings. A sociologist interviewed black customers and came to this conclusion:[41]

They said the Chinese were clever, reserved merchants who made profits from high-priced groceries. Blacks are aware that the Chinese invest money in real property such as commercial buildings and houses in the black community, from which they are thought to receive large returns. On the other hand, blacks acknowledge that the Chinese merchants donate to black churches and athletic clubs.

---

[40] George A. Rummel, III, *"The Delta Chinese: An Exploratory Study in Assimilation."* Master of Arts thesis, University of Mississippi, 1966, 32.

[41] Robert Seto Quan. *Lotus Among Magnolias: The Mississippi Chinese.* (Jackson: University Press of Mississippi, 1982), 53.

He found unqualified strong positive sentiments about Chinese grocers among older blacks, as illustrated by this example.

> The Chinese and his family and kin have all been here for a long, long time. We've all traded with these stores down the street since I can remember. The Chinese sold us everything we needed. Like when my wife had her first baby, the woman [midwife] sent me down to Jack's to pick up towels, aspirin, and things like that. I didn't have much money then, but Jack said I could pay him back later. We would pay up when we could, and they were friendly about it, too. We all get along here real good. The Chinese are good people.[42]

Chinese Grocers Across The Delta

Almost every town in the Delta on both sides of the Mississippi River came to have one or more Chinese grocery stores eventually. A description of the origins and operations of a cross section of these stores will serve to show many similarities in how the Chinese grocery became a part of these communities. Remarkably, virtually all Chinese in the region were engaged as grocery merchants. Such homogeneity of occupation for one ethnic group is rare, and reflects how few work opportunities were available for Chinese or how lucrative the grocery business was, or some combination of the two factors.

Marks, Ms.

Pang Jone Sam came from China before 1900. He picked up trade skills like baking in Cairo, Illinois, and carpentry in Roanoke, Virginia, before he came to the Delta where he first peddled peanuts and other goods up and down the Mississippi River. When he was 20, he

---

[42] Ibid. 54

moved from Dublin to Marks where he built and operated Sam Joe's Grocery in 1902.

Figure 18 Pang Jone Sam family in Marks, Ms., 1921. L-R Shaw, Pap, Yee, Mr. Pang holding Walter, wife Fong Shee holding Doris, King, Andy, and Gene. Courtesy, Cedric Chinn and Pang family.

Returning to China a few years later, he married and returned to Marks around 1910 with his wife and their first child, a daughter. The Pang family, which would grow to 10 children, lived behind the store on Main Street. Just before the depression in the 1930a he sent eight of the children to China to learn the Chinese language and customs. Pang, one of the earliest Chinese to have children born in the Delta, was well accepted and regarded favorably in Marks. [43] [44]

---

[43] A story of remarkable achievement; The legacy of Pang Jone Sam. *Quitman County Democrat,* May 10, 2007, 3.

Greenville, Ms.

George Seu, was born in Canton in 1912, and with his wife ran the Min Sang grocery in Greenville(See Figures 19 and 20). Established in 1934, it is the longest continuously operated grocery in Greenville, now run by his sons Jerome and Harry Seu.

Figure 19 George and Grace Seu in the Min Sang grocery in Greenville.

George Seu immigrated to the United States using the paper surname of Pang when he was thirteen to join his brother, 20 years older, to run a laundry in Chicago for a few years. When they learned of need for grocery stores for the thousands of farm laborers in the Delta, his brother left him to run the laundry and headed to Mississippi to explore prospects in the grocery business. He soon joined his brother in Greenville where they initially had two stores on opposite corners of the same intersection, one serving black customers and the other serving whites; later these stores were combined.

---

[44]Andrew "Andy" Pang remembers. *Quitman County Democrat*, May 10, 2007. 3.

Figure 20 Min Sang Grocery, Greenville opened in 1934 and replaced in 1952. Courtesy, Delta State University Archives, Cleveland, Ms.

As his oldest daughter Frieda Quon related:

My dad came to Chicago to join two older brothers who operated a laundry business. Even though his middle class family owned and operated a mercantile business in China, they believed greater opportunities existed in the United States or Gam San (Gold Mountain). The Chinese were under the misconception that wealth was easily attained if one simply worked hard to earn it. They had no idea of the incredible hardship, long hours of work, discrimination, prejudice and anti-Chinese sentiments that immigrants encountered. Parents did not know if or when they would ever see their children again. My father did not return to

China for sixteen years, by then his father had passed away. The intent was to earn money to send to family in China and eventually return to their homeland. Arriving as a young teenager, my father learned all the skills necessary for survival in his new environment: cooking, washing, sewing, and ironing. As was the custom, when it was time for my father to find a bride he returned to China for an arranged marriage with my mother. My mother Grace Wong, born in Brooklyn, NY was given for adoption because her birth mother did not keep girl babies. When my mother was nine, her adoptive father was murdered. Her adopted mother moved my mom and two stepbrothers to China. At the age of eighteen my mom married my father who was twenty-nine; she never met him until their wedding day. Mom and Dad would not visit China again for thirty years. Dad brought Mom to Greenville to join the family business and became parents to five children.[45]

Boyle, Ms.

Ed Joe's father came to Mississippi after working on the Pacific coast, then returning to China to get married in 1928, and returning the next year alone as his wife could not come until 1949.

... my dad came from Canton, China, at the age of ten or twelve years old. He was a houseboy on a ship that came out of China that came to the United States. He came to Seattle, Washington and from that he migrated to San Francisco. He worked as a houseboy when he as an assistant to Thomas Edison there at Stanford University. From that point, he stayed there, and studied English for several years.

He had friends that lived in Mississippi that invited him to come south. So he came across to Chicago and then down by train to Memphis to the Delta. This was in 1912, there about. One of the stories he tells back in those days is that it is more wilderness than anything else in the delta. He worked

[45]Frieda Quon. Interview by Kimberly Lancaster and Jennifer Mitchell, Jan.12, 2000. transcript, Delta State University Oral History Archives, Cleveland, Ms.

in the business there in the Boyle grocery store. They had on Saturday night there was always something going on. He told this story that they thought that it was New Years Eve. People were shooting their guns. He stepped out of the store for just a minute came out on the street and fell over. He was shot. He didn't think it was New Year's Eve then. That happens back in those days quite often.

In Boyle he stayed. Well, naturally that is where I was born. After he worked there in the grocery store for several years, then in 1928, he went back to China and married my mother. He stayed there for a year, and then came back to the business. Then in 1949, my mother came from China. [46] [47]

Rolling Fork, Ms.

Sam Jue's father started the Sam Sing grocery store in 1933 in Rolling Fork, a town of about 2500 located about 35 miles southeast of Greenville. Sam came from China as a young boy to the Delta.

After serving three years in the military with the celebrated Flying Tigers that fought so well against the Japanese during World War II, he took over the store from his father after the war and operated it with his wife Susan. Located on China Street, the store served mostly black working customers and still operated in 2008 (See Figure 21) although over the years, the number of Chinese grocery stores in town declined from four to one. [48], [49]

---

[46]Edward and Annette Joe Interview, May 1, 2000.

[47]The dates in this interview may be incorrect. Edward's brother, Peter believes his father came in 1910, returned to China in 1920 to marry, and brought his wife to the Delta in 1927. Personal communication from Peter Joe to Author, Feb. 27, 2008.

[48] Jack Joe, e-mail message to Author March 11, 2008.

[49] "Delta's Chinese groceries dwindling." *The Clarion-Ledger*, Jackson, Ms., Aug. 8, 2005.

Figure 21 Sam Sing grocery in Rolling Fork, Ms.

Hollandale, Ms.

Bobby Jue grew up in Hollandale and remembers stories about his grandfather coming to the U. S. from China.

> Well, what I heard was that my grandfather came over first. He worked out on a railroad in California. Somehow he came down here and wound up in Arkansas first. Then he ended up in Mayersville, Mississippi. He had a grocery store there. Then my father, I still have an old key chain that he had, that he dated back in 1937. I heard he came around the mid thirties about '35. He came first. He had a store in Rolling Fork, which is about ten miles from Mayersville. Then from there he went to Greenville. He had a store on Lake St. in Greenville. From Greenville, he came to Hollandale.[50]

Hollandale was a small town that had only a few Chinese, so the community was more willing to accept Chinese. And as the number of

---

[50]Bobby and Laura Jue. Interview by Kimberly Lancaster, Feb. 4, 2000, transcript, Delta State University Oral History Archives, Cleveland, Ms.

Chinese there grew to about 50, Hollandale eventually had as many as seven Chinese grocery stores, but now only 1 or 2 are left.

> Before he (father) came to Hollandale (from Greenville), he didn't know if the school officials or the mayor would let us go to school here. My brother was one year older than I am. Then I had a sister. My sister was born here in Hollandale. He had to make sure we could go to school here before he built a store. So got approved that we could go to school here. So bought a lot across. Well... what we would call across the tracks. He built the store there in 1948...I think a thousand square foot. It might have been eight hundred or thousand square foot.[51]

Unfortunately, his father died when Bobby was only six, but a brother-in-law from Vicksburg came to help his mother run the business, Jue's Grocery, which operated for 27 years.

Louise, Ms.

Lee Hong came over in 1917 to San Francisco. He planned to head for Chicago after he earned enough to pay off his passage, but a cousin in Louise, Ms. urged him to come instead to the Delta where he entered the grocery business. Lee Hong knew English and was a successful businessman who built the Lee Hong Theater next to his grocery. Blacks, being more numerous than whites, sat downstairs while whites occupied the balcony.

In 1960 Lee Hong retired, and his third son, Hoover, took over the store. Hoover came to the U. S. at 9 mo. of age in 1934, and was named after the U.S.S. Hoover on which he arrived. On special occasions the family might visit other Chinese in nearby towns, but otherwise they were isolated from other Chinese but were aware of relevant issues for

---

[51]Interview Bobby Jue and Laura Jue. Feb. 4, 2000

Chinese through a subscription to the Chinese newspaper from San Francisco. Hoover attended Port Gibson military academy for 2 middle school years. He went on to attend college at Mississippi State University before he served in the military. He later served as mayor of Louise from 1973-1997 and served for many years on the City Council.

Hoover's wife, Freeda, came from Ruleville, where her father also ran a grocery business. In Louise, with only 1 or 2 Chinese, there was no problem of their children attending white schools. The Lees learned that joining the Methodist church gained them better acceptance by white society.

Hoover's older brother, John, met his wife (Sacramento born) during a visit to China. He brought her to Mississippi where he acquired a grocery business. Operating a store was demanding. For example, to get meat, he would drive a pickup truck to a farm to buy a steer. He had to shoot and butcher it to have meat to bring to the store for sale. Among his wife's store duties was repackaging food items purchased in bulk into smaller quantities for sale to customers.

The store was small, and the family lived in crowded quarters in the back of store. A butcher table had to double up as a bed at night by placing a mattress over it. Eventually, life proved too unpleasant for his wife working in the grocery and raising 4 children in Louise. At her insistence, John decided to relocate his family to Phoenix, Az.[52]

Clarksdale, Ms.

Penny Gong's parents worked in San Francisco, where they were having a difficult time earning a living. A relative from the Delta visiting

---

[52] Hoover Lee, Telephone interview by John Jung, Aug. 16, 2007.

them in the early 1950s urged them to move to Mississippi when they would be better off financially operating a grocery store.

> My mother was born in California in 1922, and my father was born in China. He came over to the United States when he was eight years old. He and my mother were married in 1944, and in 1954 we moved to Mississippi (from San Francisco).
>
> My father had a great aunt that lived in Boyle, Ms., and she said this was the land of opportunity. So my father picked up his family, and we moved to Cleveland. We stayed here a year. We had a store on Highway 61. At that time there was not that much traffic. We had a grocery store. My parents could not make it. So my grandfather had a friend in Clarksdale, thirty-six miles away from here. He took my father under his wing, and set us up with a grocery store in Clarksdale, and that is where we all resided...it was very hard for my brother and sister when we moved here. Both of them failed the first year because of the language differences, the accents, and the differences in the schools from California. Both my brother and sister really never liked it here in Mississippi. As soon as they graduated from Delta State, they moved back to California.[53]

Altheimer, Arkansas

Leland Gion grew up in Altheimer, Arkansas, a small cotton plantation town, where his parents operated a grocery store, Benson & Co., shown in Figure 22. His grandfather and a cousin established the business before his father, Jue Book Gion, came from China in the 1920s. Although his true surname was Joe or Chow, it was recorded as Gion because the order of Chinese names, which is the reverse of sequence for

---

[53]Penny Gong Interview by Georgene Clark, Oct. 7, 1999, transcript, Delta State University Oral History Archives, Cleveland, Ms.

American names, confused the immigration officer.

Like many Chinese immigrants, he came over as a bachelor but he did not return to China to marry as his wife was born in California. They lived in the back of the store. Leland recalled that living conditions were quite spartan, as they had to use an outhouse until he was 9 or 10.

There were only three Chinese families in Altheimer so they were easily accepted in the community. Unlike in Mississippi, Chinese were allowed to attend white schools and many of his childhood playmates were white schoolmates. When white neighbors offered to pick him up and transport him, his parents allowed him to attend Sunday school. However, his parents did not emphasize or encourage religious and church participation.[54]

Figure 22 Benson & Co. store in Altheimer, Arkansas. c. 1930s. Library of Congress LC-USF33-011695-M2.

---

[54] Leland Gion Interview with John Jung, Oct. 26, 2007.

Earle, Arkansas

Audrey Sidney was born in St. Louis, Missouri in 1934. She recalled her parents' grocery store in Earle, Arkansas, a town of about 3,000.

> I grew up in Earle, Arkansas, which is in Crittenden County, across the Mississippi River near Memphis, Tennessee. My parents moved from St. Louis where they were in the laundry business. They entered into the grocery business. They moved in 1937 to Earle, Arkansas. I come from a family that had eight children. There are five girls and three boys [in our family]. He not only had two grocery stores, one at Earle, Arkansas, and the other at Black Fish Lake, which was on Highway 70, but he also had a farm. I am not sure of their level of education. They are immigrants from the Canton, (Guangdong) China area. The United States was the land of opportunity; thus, they came to the U.S. to make more money, and then hopefully go back to China, which they were never able to do. I am not sure when they were married. The (Chinese) families would invest their money in the store. It would be a family enterprise. They lived in the back of the store. Sometimes it would be three people sharing a bed, if it was a large family…we did not have a lot of frills…The main thing that we knew was how (to do is) to work [in the store] and have the determination to succeed.[55]

White Attitudes Toward Early Chinese Grocers

Over the years, white attitudes toward Chinese grocers improved substantially, but in earlier times there were mixed, and sometimes, hostile views as expressed by a white merchant in a large town.[56]

---

[55]Audrey Sidney Interview by Kimberly Lancaster, Feb. 4, 2000, transcript, Delta State University Oral History Archives, Cleveland, Ms.

[56] Rummel, "Delta Chinese,"34. Some Delta Chinese took strong exception to these white perceptions, which they felt were invalid, based on their experience and furthermore should not be reported because they would kindle racial ill-feelings. Some felt that even if some whites had such perceptions, it was long ago and did not reflect the

The Chinese here are real funny, some of the richest and most respected members of this community are Chinese and yet some of the worst people here are the Chinese. They have some of the finest stores here in [Community] and they also have some of the worst stores. If they have the big stores like the [Super Duper] Supermarket out on the highway you couldn't find a better store to trade in. They believe in competition and every member of the family works in that store but when you look at the Chinese stores down by the river, you get a totally different picture. They're right down in n----- town and what goes on there, God only knows.

When those yellow people first came here, nobody really knew what to think, but some of them have proved themselves and we've accepted them but those that stayed down with the n----, well, we just let them go. What they do is their own business. I wouldn't mind having one of those [Chinese Merchants] living next to me, but some of those that live along the river, why I would move before they came in.

In smaller towns where there were only a few Chinese, individual grocers were able to forge more harmonious relationships with whites in the community. Realizing their lower status, the Chinese knew they had to gain the acceptance of influential whites that controlled the community even if they had to sometimes be exceedingly polite and solicitous toward them. One Chinese who grew up in North Dakota and came to the Delta in 1939 immediately noticed this strategy in operation.

What struck me most upon arriving in Mississippi was the deferential etiquette my brother-in-law and his father displayed toward the white elite. It impressed me and my other two sisters, who had just arrived from China, so much that whenever we saw certain whites approaching the store we would franticly look for my brother-in-law or his father

present. In general, Delta Chinese I met were sensitive about race relations, which they were reluctant to discuss. They do not dwell on the past and want to move ahead.

because to let anybody other than the boss wait on these customers would be lacking in respect.[57]

He further observed how his brother-in-law focused on cultivating relationships with influential whites such as town fathers, higher-ups in the grocery wholesale houses, and immigration officers. Using this approach he was able to get the town's Chinese admitted to the white public school, secure loans for relatives to start a new business, and bring relatives from China.

Over the years this family gained the respect of the town's whites. A noteworthy instance occurred in 1968 when a white man, known for his strong anti-Chinese stance in earlier years, wrote a letter of complaint to a Greenville judge. During an organized boycott of the Delta retail stores, blacks were blocking the entrance to a Chinese grocery store run by a family that he highly praised.[58]

Conclusion

The stories of how these Chinese immigrants came to be in the Delta to operate grocery stores have a remarkable similarity. Although the details of dates and specific towns differ, there is a common pattern in the journeys that they took from nearby villages in Guangdong to the United States. Most first worked in other regions of the country, but had relatives in the Delta who encouraged and assisted them to come work in

---

[57] Paul Wong, e-mail message to Author, March 5, 2008.

[58] Ibid. The complexity of race relations is illustrated by the fact that since the grocer died in 1999, his family has contributed over $100,000 to Teach for America, a national nonprofit organization that provides scholarships to college students to teach for a year or two in inner city schools.

grocery stores. Through the help of relatives, each newcomer to the region eventually was able to save enough to start his own store.

Most came to the United States before marrying, but after working a few years returned to China to find a wife. There were few Chinese women, single or married, in the United States during the exclusion law years. Arrangements for a suitable match were made through a matchmaker or by parents and relatives. Some men were able to bring wives, and even families over, but others could not afford the costs or obtain necessary documents for bringing families here. They had to make periodic return visits to see their wives and children until some eventually succeeded in bringing their families during the 1920s, or later when some restrictions ended.

Once here, the grocer and his family worked together to develop their business. They spent long hours in the store each day and many lived behind or near their stores. Everyone had a role to play in the operation of the business. Children and older women often stocked shelves and repackaged bulk quantities of food items into smaller sizes. Some older children were involved with tasks of cutting meat or making deliveries on bicycle. Grandparents, if they lived in the store, also helped in various ways in addition to watching after younger children and preparing meals.

4. Chain Migration to the Delta

A better appreciation of the intricate paths that the Chinese took in reaching the Delta can be obtained by examining several examples that illustrate the interconnections among relatives that were essential to the successful migration to the South from Guangdong villages and distant parts of the United States. The details and methods varied somewhat across individuals, but their stories all demonstrate how committed networks of family members played vital roles in helping newcomers succeed in finding their way to the Delta to make their living operating a grocery store.

An Example of Chain Migration in Greenville

One of the first Chinese grocery stores to operate in the Delta opened in the 1890s in Greenville, with a prominent location right next to the levee at the foot of Washington St. As the photograph on the front cover of this book shows, the store was a popular place for customers to congregate and socialize.

The store served as the foundation for a chain of migration of Chinese to work in grocery stores in the area, as summarized in Figure 23. Around 1910, the owner, Joe Gow Nue, decided to retire, sell his store, and return to China. At this time, three brothers, Joe Nam, Joe King, and Joe Guay were running a laundry in Holyoke, Ma. They had assistance coming to the U. S. from another brother, Joe Yuke, who had worked on railroad construction in Montana before moving to Sacramento, Ca. The youngest one, Joe Guay came in 1902 to Vancouver, crossed Canada, and entered illegally at the border town of Ogdensburg, New York. However, he and about 20 or more other Chinese were quickly apprehended, arrested, and jailed. Somehow, his brother Joe Nam with the aid of an attorney convinced the court that Joe Guay was a returning U. S. citizen by birth.

These brothers may have learned about the Delta grocery business opportunity because they originated from the same village, Wang Sek, in Hoiping from where Joe Gow Nue came. They believed that running a grocery would be easier work than operating a laundry and purchased the store, retaining the store's original name.

The youngest brother, Joe Guay, remained in Massachusetts to run the Holyoke laundry. But after a few years, he joined his brothers in Greenville in the early 1920s. His oldest son, Joe Young, remained in Massachusetts to attend MIT where he obtained a civil engineering degree. He then left to China to work, first on a railroad, and then on various commercial and industrial structures. During the latter stages of the war with Japan he was drawn into working for the Chinese government on war-related projects, achieving the rank of Colonel.

Around 1924, the two older brothers, Joe Nam and Joe King retired to return to Guangdong, leaving Joe Guay to operate the Joe Gow Nue grocery store. As the grocery business expanded, he needed help. As many other Chinese grocers did, he arranged for some distant cousins from China, Joe Duck-fue and Joe Duck-kong, to immigrate and help with the work. They were housed and fed in the back of the store.[59]

---

[59] Helen Wong, "Through my eyes: A family history." Unpublished, 2007.

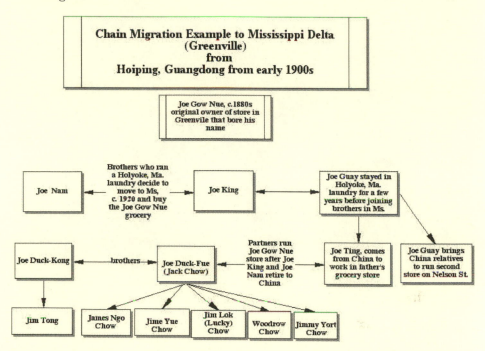

Figure 23 Chain Migration of the Joe family to Greenville, Ms.

In addition to stocking the typical food items found in other grocery stores, the Joe Gow Nue store also carried a variety of imported Chinese food ingredients, Chinese art objects, and Chinese cultural items ordered from China or San Francisco merchants. This merchandise attracted business from the Chinese throughout the region, and the Joe Gow Nue store became like a travel agency that helped Chinese immigrants with travel tickets, immigration forms, and passport applications. Success led later to opening of a second store on Nelson St. in 1935 (See Figure 24) with the help of Joe Duck-Fue and his family.

Figure 24 Joe Gow Nue Market #2, Nelson Street, Greenville c. 1940 Courtesy, Dick Ming Joe.

Joe Ting, a second son of Joe Guay, shown in Figure 25 with his father came to Greenville in 1927 to help with the store. Because Chinese were not allowed to attend white schools in Greenville, Joe Ting attended high school in Sacramento, California and then classes at a business school in Memphis. Joe Ting was a successful businessman and he also learned how to sell life insurance to other Chinese. He became a leader and spokesperson for the Chinese in Greenville. He recognized the advantages to be gained by working with local churches interested in attracting Chinese and he helped persuade many Chinese to attend the Baptist church. With other grocers in Cleveland and other Delta towns, he also helped raise funds for the Cleveland Baptist Church to set up a Chinese school in 1934 that will be discussed further in Chapter 6.[60]

---

[60]Joe Ting was a major source of information for James Loewen, Robert Seto Quan, and Ted Shepherd, authors of three prior historical accounts of the Delta Chinese grocers.

Figure 25 Joe Ting (standing) and his father, Joe Guay (seated) in the Joe Gow Nue Grocery Store in Greenville, Ms. From the Joe Ting Collection.

During the 1940s several other male cousins including Joe Duck-Wing, Lucky Chow, Yick Joe, Wai Chow, Jim Tong, and James Ngo Chow, came to the region to work in the expanding grocery business. However, in 1945, Joe Guay, the last of the original brothers who developed the store died. In 1947 the remaining partners decided to divide their properties. Joe Ting assumed control of the Washington St. store while Joe Duck-fue with help of James Ngo Chow managed the Nelson St. store.

Lucky Chow, whose father had been a partner in the Joe Gow Nue grocery store, opened his own grocery store in 1955 in a poor section of Greenville at the corner of Theobald and Clay Streets. A few years later, he opened a large market at Alexander and Kentucky Streets. Just a couple of steps from the store, Lucky built a large red brick house for all the relatives that worked in the store. It had five rooms and two and a half baths with a very large living room, large kitchen, and a dining room.

They grew Chinese vegetables in the large back yard. At one time there were five families with a total of 18 persons living in the house including Uncle Ling, a butcher, Pang the produce manager, cashier and stocker, and Uncle Woodrow who ordered groceries.

After the war between Japan and China, and the collapse of the Nationalist government of Chiang Kai Shek in 1949, Joe Young, the eldest son of Joe Guay, who as mentioned earlier had been working as a civil engineer in China, decided it best to return with his wife and children to the U.S. Although he had a civil engineering degree from MIT, a highly prominent university, no one would hire a Chinese as an engineer in those days. Seeing how Chinese with much less education were successful in the grocery business and able to send their children to college, he opened a grocery store first in Tchula, and then in Greenville in 1960.

The Joe Gow Nue store building, which survived the great flood of 1927 that devastated the Delta, was later sold to a law firm after the family elders retired. However, a fire destroyed the venerable landmark in 1998. The historic site was then reduced to serving as a parking lot for riverboat casinos by the levee at the end of Washington Street.[61] But, for over half a century, the building housed a prosperous business for the Joe brothers and their families in Greenville that provided valued service to the community and to Chinese throughout the region.

Chain Migration: Clarksdale, Boyle, and Cleveland

Born in Hoiping about 1889, Jew Guey Moon came to the U. S. in or around 1908 arriving in San Francisco. His purchased identity

---

[61] Dick Ming Joe, e-mail message to Paul Wong, March 18, 2008.

papers were those that belonged to a 10 year old son of Jew Moy, a partner in the Quong Hong Sing Co., a store in Merced, Ca. However, he was not admitted into the U. S. on this attempt because he had an eye infection (trachoma).

Undaunted by this unexpected setback that cost him $1500, he was determined to make a new effort. After he saved the same amount of money to try again, Guey Moon finally succeeded in gaining entry at San Francisco in August, 1909, with the aid of a prominent attorney, Oliver P. Stidger who specialized in handling Chinese immigration cases. Being small in stature, even though he was 21 years old on his second try, Guey Moon was able to pass as the 10 year old identified on his purchased papers who would have been only 12 or 13 by this date.

He found work on farms and ranches for $16.50/month plus room and board, in the Sacramento, California, area not far from the Sierra mountains, known to the Chinese as the fabled Gold Mountain. He found work for a white family and lived in their home where he slept in a spare room and ate his meals with them. Working all day in the fields with them, he acquired horticultural skills grafting fruit and nut trees. The farm owner's wife, interested in helping Guey, taught him English after dinner using newspapers. After he achieved a good command of English, he decided to improve his station in life. He moved to work in the sawmills around Lodi and later found employment on the Tonopah and Tidewater Railroad in northern California and Nevada where he learned to be a cook.

About 1911 he, and several kinsmen from Gor Doi village in Hoiping like Jew Dow Lin and his son Jew Hen Lett, each purchased a

$1,000 partnership in the Sun On Chong Co. in Sacramento, Ca. This investment was important because it established them as merchants (See Figure 26), which was more fiction than truth, but would be useful later to bring families over.

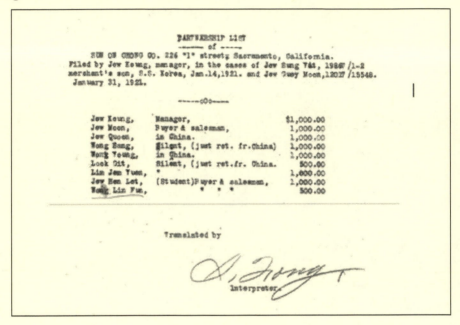

Figure 26 Jew Guey Moon purchased a share of a company in Sacramento, Ca. that conferred merchant status to him.

At the time he was working in the agricultural region of northern California, several of his kinsmen from the same village in China had already immigrated to Mississippi. The Joe family relatives worked as partners in a company they formed in the 1920s, Joe Brothers, that operated several grocery stores in the area around Cleveland, Boyle, and Clarksdale to the north of Greenville, as outlined in Figure 27. These village cousins sought other relatives to work in their booming and growing retail and wholesale grocery business. They persuaded Guey Moon about 1926 that having a grocery business was a lucrative opportunity for earning a livelihood and invited him to join them in the Delta.

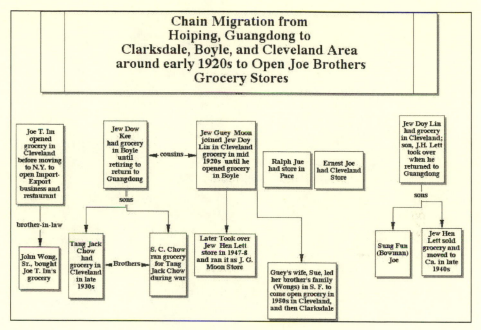

Figure 27 Chain Migration of Joe Brothers in Clarksdale, Boyle, Cleveland area.

Jew Guey Moon took this opportunity to improve his economic lot and moved to Cleveland to help with the grocery stores. He returned in 1920 to China to be married in an arranged match. He saw his bride for the first time at the wedding. Over the next decade, he started his family with several returns to the village when he fathered 2 children. In Mississippi, he earned and sent money home regularly to support his family and build a house for them. However, his wife died during childbirth of a third child. Guey returned in 1935 and remarried the next year in an arranged match to Wong Shee with whom he had a daughter, Lillie. In 1939, Wong Shee came to the U. S. with Lillie, her half-sister

Sue King, and an adopted son Joe Sing just ahead of the outbreak of World War II.

Figure 28 Joe Brothers Grocery Store, Cleveland, Ms. Courtesy, Sung Gay Chow.

The Joe Brothers store (See Figure 28) served poorer white, and black customers whereas another store catered mainly to white customers that were more affluent (See Figures 29 and 30). Operating under the name, Modern Stores, an unorthodox name for a grocery store, it was intended to attract a different clientele than an ordinary or plain store would. Located only a few doors away on the same block of Sharpe Street in the main business section of Cleveland, with its attractive window displays of merchandise Modern was a clean and tidy store that could compete with the best of the white-owned stores.

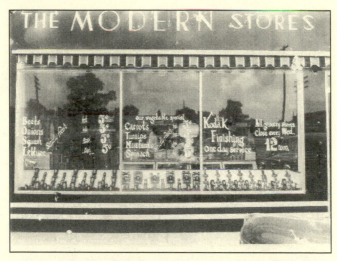

Figure 29 Exterior of Modern Stores Cleveland, Ms. Courtesy of Sung Gay Chow

Figure 30 Interior of Modern Stores. Tang Jack Chow, store manager, standing between a nephew, Chester Chow, and employee, Jimmy Robinson. Courtesy of Sung Gay Chow .

After the war ended, more of the family members of the other Joe Brothers Co. partners were reunited in the Delta allowing them to expand by opening several more stores in the region. The family partners even shared a large house aptly named the Joe Brothers house (See Figure 31).

Figure 31 The multi-family house for the Joe Brothers. Courtesy, Sung Gay Chow

Located within walking distance to the grocery stores, it was large enough to provide living quarters for six couples or small families downstairs and several rooms upstairs for partners who were bachelors. The partners held large family gatherings for special occasions like Thanksgiving and Christmas each year. Each partner eventually bought their own homes when they were able to bring their families from China.

Figure 32 J. G. Moon grocery store in Boyle Ms. Courtesy of Bobby Joe Moon

Eventually, as conditions changed, Joe Bros. Co. slowly dissolved. Some grocers retired and moved to other parts of the country or went back to China. Guey took over the store in Boyle shown in Figure 32, and other partners operated various other locations. Guey ended up with the original Joe Bros. Co. store in Cleveland, which later was rented out for many years until his death.[62]

Chain Migration to The Arkansas Delta

The route from Guangdong to Arkansas was rather circuitous for members of the Chu, Wong, and Low families. Figure 33 shows the complex path that the Chu family took from running laundries in Michigan and Illinois before entering the grocery business in rural Arkansas. The diagram also illustrates the trail of two other families, the Wongs and Lows, also involved with operating grocery stores on the Arkansas side of the Delta.[63] Eventually several marriages occurred among children from these families as well as to other Chinese, all of whom operated grocery stores in Arkansas.

The Chu Family

Several families, as Figure 33 illustrates, starting from different parts of the U. S. converged on the Arkansas side of the river to operate grocery stores. Eventually, marriages between members of these families strengthened the ties among them.

Chu Kwok Kin came alone to the U. S. in the late 1890s leaving his wife in the village. However, he was denied entry but became a

---

[62]I am indebted to Bobby Joe Moon for providing details of Goey Joe Moon's life history.
[63]I am indebted to Henry Wong, Gow Sek Low, and Don Chu for supplying details of the Delta interconnections among their families.

contract worker on a Mexican railroad until he gained legal entry into the
U. S. in 1903 when he worked in laundries.

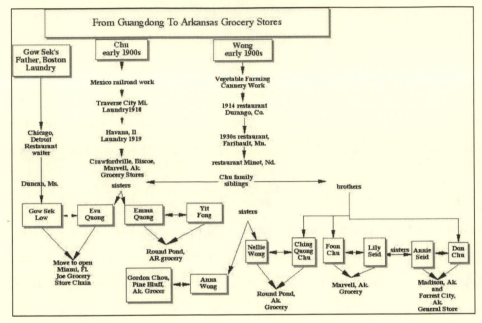

Figure 33 Migration Chain of 3 grocery families to the Arkansas side of the Delta

He had been away for almost 10 years before his wife heard from
him again. Finally he was able to return to the village in 1915 and this
time, with his wife, they crossed Canada, entering the U. S. at New York.
In 1918, he purchased a laundry in Traverse City, Michigan but then
moved the next year to open another one in Havana, Illinois. During the
Depression, business was so bad that he sent his family back to China to
live with relatives for a few years but not before he arranged a match for
his oldest daughter, Emma, to marry Yit Fong, so she could remain in the
U. S. Yit was the son of a family friend from their village, Jook Wan. He
operated a grocery store in Round Pond, Arkansas and later one in
Hughes.

Around 1934, Chu Kwok planned a trip to China to join his family and decided to visit Emma and Yit before he departed. They persuaded him to stay in Arkansas and establish a grocery store in Crawfordville with the aid of a young nephew. Chu Kwok soon found better grocery opportunities in Biscoe, and later in Marvell, but needed to have his two oldest sons, Foon and Ching, come back from China to help.

Concerned about the impending war with Japan, he decided it was time to bring the rest of the family back to the U. S. However, his wife had no visa and the decision was made to send the two youngest children, Eva and Don, back to the U.S. by themselves. Finally, at the last moment, a visa was obtained, and the oldest son, Ching, returned to the village to escort his mother back. While he was there, he was introduced to Nellie Wong as a prospective wife. They married in 1940 just before they came back to the U. S. They went to Round Pond, Ark. to run a grocery store, as will be described in more detail in the section on the Wong family. Later, Nellie's younger sister, Anna, married Gordon Chou, whose parents had immigrated from Hoiping, Guangdong to Pine Bluff, Arkansas where they operated a grocery.

Before long, Chu's two other sons, Foon and Don, each married a sister from a Seid family from Portland, Oregon. In 1940, Foon Chu married Lily Seid and they settled in Forrest City, Arkansas where they operated a hardware and jewelry store. A decade later, in 1951, Foon's younger brother Don married Lily's younger sister, Annie. They came to the Delta and operated a grocery in Madison, Arkansas from about 1950-1960. They left the grocery business and moved to Forrest City, Arkansas, where Don worked as a jeweler and did watch repairs before retiring there. The Seid sisters' older brother, Bing, operated a grocery in Crawfordville for many years before moving to Memphis.

The Wong Family

Nellie's father, Lim Sing Wong, had first immigrated to the United States alone in 1901, leaving his wife behind in the village in Guangdong. In his early 20's, he entered the U. S. at Seattle working on vegetable farms in the region before contracting to work briefly in Alaska on a sea going salmon cannery. He did not find this work to his liking so he worked as a cook in the Pacific Northwest with an uncle. After working several years he managed to save enough to return to China to marry Mah Bo-Nui. Soon he came back to the U.S. and around 1914 he and his uncle had a restaurant in Durango, Colorado to serve copper mine workers. After World War I ended, copper mining declined so they left the region. Wong returned to China to be with his wife and two sons, but around 1921, he brought his wife and youngest son to the U. S. and opened a restaurant in Faribault, Minnesota. There were no other Chinese in the area, and not speaking English, his wife was especially isolated. She did not encounter another Chinese woman for 10 years after she arrived there until a Chinese couple traveling through town happened to dine at their restaurant.[64]

After a few years there, the family, then with three sons, moved to North Dakota, to operate a restaurant in Minot located on the Great Northern and Soo Railroad route. When the Depression hit in the 1930s, business was so poor that in 1931 they decided to return to China. Those were the circumstances when Nellie entered the earlier described marriage

---

[64] Henry Wong, e-mail message to Author, March 24, 2008.

match to Chu Ching Quong from Arkansas. The newly weds left for the U. S. on one of the last ships to leave Hong Kong before the war, bringing along her younger brother Henry and sister Anna. They went to Round Pond, Arkansas, where Chu Ching's father operated a grocery store.

Living in Arkansas was an isolating existence for them with so few Chinese in the region. Life in Round Pond was also physically uncomfortable. They had no running water and had to use a hand pump to obtain water, which was rather dirty looking. They had no indoor toilets and used outhouses for many years. There were only a few other Chinese in the region, but their contact was limited as they were several miles away.

Nellie and her husband operated a general store for 41 years in Round Pond, a town that was so small that it did not survive and today no longer exists. During their years in Round Pond, Chu Ching earned the distinction in 1957 of becoming the first Chinese American Post Master, a position he held for 24 years. In addition to selling groceries at their store, they also carried many small hardware items. They also acquired some farmland that they rented to tenants who raised cotton, soybeans, and wheat.

Chinese in these rural areas kept informed about issues related to China through subscriptions to Chinese newspapers mailed from San Francisco or New York, as the few Chinese living in Arkansas were scattered by miles. Few owned cars, nor did they have much free time, as they were often working until midnight and stayed open 7 days a week all year round. Operating a store in rural Arkansas was dangerous. They were robbed at gunpoint on one occasion, and a neighbor was raped in another incident. They finally gave up their business in 1981 because of the heightened dangers of crimes perpetrated by blacks against Chinese merchants.

There are even fewer Chinese in Arkansas now, as many of the children moved away after they grew up to seek employment in white collar and professional occupations. For example, Don and Annie (from same village in China) have 2 sons in Memphis about 50 miles away, another in California, and one in Kentucky.

The Low Family

Eva Quong, Emma's younger sister, married Gow Sek Low, whose father came over from China around 1900 to Boston where he first worked in a laundry before having a succession of jobs as a waiter in restaurants in New York, Detroit, and Chicago. A friend with a grocery store in Duncan, Ms. asked Gow's father to come help there. Soon after, he then went to Miami to help a friend with a laundry in 1926, but instead started his own grocery store, Joe's Markets. He was so successful that he was able to expand, eventually having 38 branch stores in Miami and other areas in Florida.

Conclusion

These examples of Delta Chinese grocers demonstrate the key role played by family networks among these immigrants. Without the assistance and collaboration from others, it would have been very much more difficult for individual grocers to get started, survive, and eventually achieve success. Sharing information, financial resources, business operations, and housing was commonplace.

Many worked in other regions of the U. S. before coming to the Delta in search of ways to earn a better living. Once there, some made numerous trips back and forth between their Guangdong villages of origin and the Delta to visit families and other relatives. The complex pattern of immigration, migration, and remigration attests to their determination and resourcefulness as they struggled with few financial assets, poor command of English, and lack of family contact. Living in an often-hostile community, they faced cultural and social isolation that required enduring courage and resolve.

5. Life in Chinese Grocery Stores

The course of a typical day in the life of a Chinese grocery store followed a regular pattern. A predictable ebb and flow of customer and grocer activities occurred in a store over the course of the weekdays from the moment the store opened in the early morning until it finally closed late at night. On weekdays, grocers had to rise early to be ready to open their stores for the black cotton field hands on their way to work. At peak hours around breakfast, lunch, and dinnertime, the grocers and their help, usually family members, had their hands full waiting on customers who often came in droves. During lulls in customer demand, they did not have much rest, as there were many tasks to perform behind the scenes to prepare the store for the next wave of customers.

A Day in Life of A Chinese Grocery Store

> ...After quickly devouring a non-cooked meal of breakfast, we put on the grocer's aprons and started working. We first put the cash trays in the cash register, making sure there were enough coins for change. We then took out the fresh vegetables and fruits from the refrigerators, displayed them on the produce shelves, removed the withered parts, and discarded badly over-ripened fruits. We always saved the not so badly over-ripened ones for ourselves ... Many times, my father drove to the produce markets before 5 a.m. to get fresh vegetables and watermelons.
>
> As soon as the store opened, the customers, many of them shoeless housewives not even freshened up or properly dressed, rushed in to buy breakfast food such as breads, milk, cereals or donuts. Around 8 a.m. day laborers came

to buy cigarette, matches, chewing gums, and other daily needs. School children bought school supplies, candies, and chewing gums ... they would sharpen their pencils, as they had no pencil sharpener at home.

After about 8:30 a.m., the deliverymen and salesmen of breads, milk, soft drinks, and pastries came, and we returned the day-old breads and empty milk and soft drink bottles to them. We stocked soft drinks in the icebox and other grocery items on the shelves. The price for each can or box must be hand marked, as we did not have those fancy mechanical labelers for marking prices.

From 9 to 11 a.m.... salesmen of all kinds came to take orders, talk about current business situations, price fluctuations, new products, and so forth. These salesmen came once a week. Some of them were not trustworthy, as they secretly cheated on the prices, sold poor quality items, added special conditions for purchases, withheld good quality products from us, or spread false rumors about business conditions. Our store was rather small, but we usually dealt with two or more dealers for the same kind of merchandise. In this way, we could compare prices and quality, and negotiated terms of purchasing. Also, we deliberately let the salesmen know that we dealt with other wholesalers so that they would have to compete with the others and would dare not cheat us too much and too often.

Starting at 11 a.m., people came to buy food for lunch, mainly cold cuts, breads, milk, small pastries, soft drinks, and, occasionally fresh fruits which were quite expensive to them. From noon to about 1 p.m., a group of laborers from the warehouses came to have lunch in our store. They bought lunchmeats, loose crackers, milk, and soft drinks. (Our customers drank a lot of soft drinks. Double Cola was the best seller.) They just sat down on the floor and ate, crowding the place and making loud noises...

...They had only half an hour for lunch and our place was small. As soon as a group of diners finished eating, they had to leave to make room for the latecomers. These diners left a heap of debris - paper napkins, paper wrappings, fruit peels, empty bottles, cigarette butts, and so forth. They did not believe in using or bother to use the garbage cans. We had to clean up after them later.

When they were all gone, we re-stocked the iceboxes for soft drinks and took turn to eat our lunch, which, again, was just simple food that required no cooking. From 1 to 3 p.m. the store usually was quiet; only a few customers and salesmen would be around. This was when the wholesalers delivered their groceries, meats, dry goods, soft drinks, and many others. We checked every delivery for accuracy in prices and quantities, stored or re-stocked them, and marked prices. A few times when certain items were sold out and we forgot to re-order them or the delivery was late, we had to go to the wholesalers or suppliers to get them. It would be a luxury when we had time to take turns to nap, shop, or read during these hours.

At about 3:30 p.m. when the school children returned home, they came to the store to buy candies, bubble gums, and chewing gums. Those who had no money would still come with the hope of receiving a few pieces of the goodies from the wealthier ones.

At 4 o'clock, business picked up quickly, as the housewives came to buy food for supper. Most poor blacks had no electricity at home and, therefore, no refrigerators. They must buy perishables everyday or even every meal. They bought eggs one at a time, not a dozen. The day laborers that finished their work also came around to buy cigarettes, beer, soft drinks, and daily needs. The period from 4 to 6 p.m. was the busiest in a day.

After 6 p.m., the customers gradually thinned out and went home to eat supper. We took the unsold produce to a refrigerator to keep them fresh. We then cleaned the produce shelves, set the left-over breads aside for the bread men to take them back next morning, and added soft drinks and beer to the ice boxes.

When people finished their supper, normally after 8 p.m., many of them came to the store to chat or just stand around. Some stores provided benches for them to sit down. Our store had a little recess on the window outside for people to lean on. They would buy soft drinks, watermelon cutups, cigarettes, beer, candies, snuff, and so forth. We sometimes chatted with them. A few of them bought toys for their children or bought playing cards to play. The drunks yelled loud insults to each other and sang black folk songs. Youngsters flirted with the opposite sex…As these people had no telephone at home, they borrowed our only one in the store to make calls. The children listened to the music from our single radio and danced solo with the music, inside and outside our store.

…We closed at 8 p.m. Hungry and tired, we yet had to record the sales from the cash register, put the cash in the safe, sweep the floor, lock the doors and turn off the lights. Meanwhile, my father cooked dinner in the kitchen, using whatever that was not sold or hard to sell. (I remember one time we had ordered too much beef for steaks and could not sell all of them. We wound up with eating steaks every night for a week.) This was the only real meal we had in the whole day…Next morning we got up at 6 a.m. and repeated the same weekday routine. [65]

Weekends involved a different pattern of activity in the store with different demands on the grocers and their families.

---

[65] Zhou Liang, "Life of a Chinese American Grocer in the South."

Friday evenings in the store were quite different because most
workers got paid on that day.

> They cashed their paychecks in our store, paid part of their
> debts (90 percent of them had never-ending debts), and
> bought stuff. Now that they had money, they could afford
> to buy those costly items such as cakes and cosmetics that
> they avoided in other times. Many men went to the liquor
> store two doors down and bought whatever they fancied.
> When they got drunk, they came to our store to make
> troubles. They dared not make troubles in the two other
> stores and the gasoline station, because white men owned
> these stores and the drunken blacks would certainly be
> kicked out of the places in no time. The way we handled
> the drunks was simply to ignore or avoid them, and they
> would eventually leave us alone or, even better, leave the
> store.
>
> Saturdays were different from the weekdays. There was no
> school for children and no work for the blacks on
> Saturdays...Saturday business was always the best of the
> week, generally equal to 50 to 60 percent of the weekly
> take. Saturday was also the busiest and most tiring day.
> Our store opened at 7 a.m. and closed at 10 p.m. for the
> convenience of the customers. Since we did not open on
> Sundays and the blacks had no refrigerator at home, they
> must buy the perishable milk, eggs, and meats just prior to
> the store closing. On Saturdays, we had no real supper -
> we gobbled whatever was available. At the end of the day,
> our bodies and brains were dead tired.[66]

Sundays afforded a bit of rest for grocery families, but
not entirely because there was much maintenance, cleaning, and
preparation to be done for the upcoming week when the cycle
would repeat itself.

---

[66] Ibid.

We got up late on Sundays. Although the store was closed, we still had a lot to do, such as cleaning the refrigerators, iceboxes, produce shelves, and floors, especially the floor behind the meat counter. Everyday when we cut meat, small pieces of meat and bones fell on the floor, and that attracted mouse and roaches. Daily sweeping of the floors was really not enough; we had to do thorough washing of the floors on Sunday morning. We had to clean the streets outside the store, because the weekend drunks left many empty beer bottles and, in the summer, people threw watermelon peels on the streets.[67]

Figure 34 Chin Family Grocery, Drew, Ms. Courtesy, May Jee

Most stores opened for a few hours on Sundays, but generally closed early for church. Sundays were also spent visiting other grocery families in the same town or in nearby communities. These visits were cooperative ventures, with the adults all sharing the chores of meal preparation and cleanup, often followed by mah jong games. For the

---

[67] Ibid.

young children, these outings provided opportunities to meet and play with many other Chinese children. These gatherings helped foster bonds to a large extended family of friends that they would enjoy for many future years.[68]

Grocery Store Tasks

Running a grocery store involved more than stocking shelves and serving customers. Fresh produce had to be arranged and displayed. The grocer had to prepare orders and take deliveries from distributors and vendors to replenish the stock of goods in their family grocery and perform many tasks necessary to prepare the merchandise for sale.

> Bread vendors and dairy product vendors came every day until the 1970's when they changed to every other day. Grocery and meat deliveries were once a week. Soda drinks/beer vendors came once a week. The ice cream vendor came once a week. When the wholesalers delivered groceries, it meant pricing, stocking the shelves, and storing the remainder in the back of the store. Every Friday, meat would be cut up for display in preparation for sale on Saturday. During the week, some meat was cut as needed for sale.

In addition to the daily routines of business, operating a store involved other necessary periodic tasks.

> Every two weeks, the meat case and the drink case got a thorough washing. Each day, these cases were wiped and cleaned as needed. The floor was swept every night in preparation for the next day. Drink cases, the meat case, and shelves were restocked for the next day.[69]

---

[68] Personal communication, Luck Wing, Sept. 10, 2008.
[69] Personal communication, May Jee, May 10, 2008.

In the early days before self-service, the grocer and his family members waited on customers who had to ask for many items that were shelved behind the front counter or in glass cases.

> In the 1940's and 1950's, the merchant had to pull items from the shelves for the customer. Customers would tell my father what they wanted. My father would write the list and give it to my siblings and me to pull the groceries and box them for the customer to pick up at the end of the day. If Saturday was on the first of the month, it was extra busy because the customer would have received his wages that day and would pay his bill he accumulated from the previous month. My parents gave credit to many customers to help "tide" them over from month to month. There were also many unpaid bills at the end of the year. Therefore, my parents were basically supporting these people.[70]

In addition to retrieving and boxing purchased items, it was often necessary to deliver to the customer's residence as many lacked cars or other means of carrying them home. Although some stores had delivery trucks, others relied on bicycles for this purpose.

> Grocery delivery was always free of charge and tips were neither expected nor received. We used our only bicycle to deliver the groceries. With a basket in front and another in the back, the groceries weighed heavily, perhaps up to 50 pounds. There might be breakable glass (plastic was not common in those days) bottles, heavy cans, large flour sacks, crushable cracker boxes, squeezable tomatoes and bananas (we did not deliver eggs), meltable butter, spoilable milk and perishable meats. Fish and shrimps spoiled easily in hot weather; they must be protected against the sun. We must control the bicycle in balance so as not to let it fall. The streets in our black neighborhood were all uneven with many potholes. Some streets were just gravel roads and were hard

---

[70] Ibid.

on bicycling. When it rained, there would be flood and mud. Then we must push the bicycle through the streets. Summer in the South was usually scorching hot with the blazing sun shining on our necks. Winter could be freezing cold with icy wind blowing onto our faces. Any thin ice on the roads meant danger of falling... When we arrived to a customer's house, we had to take out each item carefully to see if there was any damage.[71]

Dealing with the delivery and salesmen required careful attention and vigilance on the part of the grocers to ensure that they received the correct goods in saleable condition.

We had to verify every bit of merchandise in our order and pay attention to any inaccuracy (wrong brand, wrong size, wrong color), omission, damage, or spoilage. Some crooked suppliers mixed inferior materials or substitutes in the deliveries, or delivered goods of lesser-known brands. We would reject those unacceptable items right on the spot. But, clever salesmen could alter or blur the writings in the sales records, deliverymen could secretly withhold part of the merchandise, or swiftly switch merchandises. We had discovered tricks after tricks in the real world of grocery business. I strongly believed that those white men deliberately intended to cheat on us Chinese, thinking they were superior to us. We Chinese Americans dared not complain [that was before the Civil Rights Act]. Once, a supplier cut us off when my father did complain.

Meat deliveries presented additional problems of spoilage if it was not quickly and properly refrigerated.

Each day, we cut just enough meat to sell. Meat cutting requires skill and experience. Steaks and chops must be cut to about equal sizes, yet not too thick and not too thin. This is not easy because the meat is soft and the bone is hard.

---

[71] Zhou Liang "Life of a Chinese American Grocer in the South"

Besides, the original pieces are all in irregular shapes. We had an electric slicer to cut lunchmeats into very thin slices. We did have a hand slicer at one time, but we discarded it as soon as we acquired the electric one. The neck bones, which were most popular among the blacks, must be chopped by an ax into small pieces for ease to cook and chew. Chickens and fish usually had their heads cut off, their internal organs removed, their skins de-feathered or scaled, and their whole bodies cleaned by the processors. So, they needed no further treatment.[72]

Store Hours of Operation

Children who grew up in the grocery store could not forget the demanding work schedule that never seemed to end until late at night, as illustrated by these recollections by several different individuals.

> Seven days, you know like Friday and Saturdays. When I come here, I don't understand why do people shop so late. Saturday night, one o'clock or two o'clock at night they come in and do their shopping. We don't get to close until two or two thirty sometimes. After we close the store. Then we have to count all the money. We don't go to bed until three o'clock. The next morning, seven thirty or eight 0' clock you get ready to open. So every Saturday night I never get enough sleep. That is how we work.[73]

> I was doing that since I was in the second or third grade. I would stay up till two or three o' clock in the morning on Saturdays helping out in the grocery store.[74]

> Five in the morning, during the growing season and harvesting season, 5:00 in the morning till, gosh, 10:00 at night. And Saturday, because they still go out in the fields on Saturday, 5:00 in the morning, but we wouldn't close until maybe 1:00 or 2:00 the next morning. And that was a rough

---

[72] Zhou Liang "Life of A Chinese American Grocer in the South."

[73] Interview Bobby and Laura Jue. Feb. 4, 2000.

[74] Ibid.

life. And there were many times that I would just fall asleep.
You know, I just didn't have the stamina, just fall asleep back
in the back with the flour. But we all pitched in and did
work.

There were certain days that we knew what we had to do.
Like Thursday all of the grocery comes in. So immediately,
with limited space, we had to stack all the grocery and put it
on the shelves. And this was the whole family doing it.
When we got out of school, the cases are piled in the aisle,
and we were expected to get up and get it out of the way. [75]

Grocery Store Merchandise

The larger stores sold more than bread, milk, eggs, cookies,
candies, soft drinks, tobacco products, and beer. Some were actually
general stores for the community and sold or rented farm and household
equipment.

We had the largest store in town (Boyle). So we had just
about everything in town. We had everything from nails to
oilcloth. We had twenty-five pounds sacks of flour. We had
garden dust. We had anything you could name. We had
washtubs. We had scrub boards. It was very much a general
store. [76]

We sold … of course, you probably don't know it (what they
are), but we called them "kneepads." When picking cotton,
they wear them because they pick cotton on their knees.
When they picked cotton they would walk on their knees all
day long. [77]

---

[75] John Paul Quon, Interview by Margaret Tullos, Dec. 2, 1999, transcript, Mississippi
Oral History Program, University of Southern Mississippi.

[76] Juanita Dong, Interview, May 1, 2000.

[77] Fay Dong, Interview by Kimberly Lancaster, May 1, 2000, transcript, Delta State
University Oral History Archives, Cleveland, Ms.

We had a general merchandise store. We sold everything. Hardware, horse feed, cow feed, and chicken feed. We had a big line of everything. We had clothes. We had material. Nuts, bolts, and screws. I learned about all of it.[78]

Figure 35 Joe Fong and his family enjoy a meal in the back of their grocery store. Courtesy, Peter Joe.

Living Quarters

The physical characteristics of the living space that many grocery families occupied were not unlike those that Shirley Hong Woo Kwan described about where her family lived behind their grocery store:

> ... in 1939 the landlord built a white shotgun house next door to the store. The store and house were connected by a screened in hallway, which served as an entrance to the house from the store. The house had three rooms used for sleeping quarters. no closets, no running water. Mom and Dad had to put nails on the walls to hang up our clothes. Mom did have a chifferobe, but that was too small to take care of everybody's clothing. Buckets of water, which we got from the store, were heated on gas heaters when we needed to wash up in the house, especially when the weather was cold.

---

[78] Lillie Woo, Interview, Feb. 14, 2000.

The warm water was poured into a wash pan for us to use. There were no toilet facilities, but we found other means to solve this problem.

In the store there was an area reserved for a small kitchen that had a stove, one sink with running water, and a bathroom. Since there was no hot water heater in the store, we had to heat the water on the stove whenever we wanted to take a bath in the deep crow's feet bathtub.[79]

We grew up in the back of a grocery store. We thought everybody lived this way, other Chinese did. We had basic necessities; crates for chairs. By today's standards we would be labeled underprivileged, but we never felt that way. We had loving parents, food, clothing, shelter; we were happy. We have fond memories playing in the stock room, our imaginary playhouse. We were sad when the wooden store was replaced with a brick store and house.[80]

So we knew there was a difference, and it was very obvious that we were ashamed to bring them in because I mean, everything was austere. We had furniture, we had chairs, but they weren't antiques, not by any means. It was functional. And if we had a big crowd to come, we would even sit on butcher-block paper (rolls) ... you know, the round rolls, we would just sit on top of them or apple crates. So, you know... makeshift type of furniture. There was no stigma among the Chinese because we were all alike.[81]

We had a house behind there...he built it connecting. I guess you would call that a house. It had a living room. Two bedrooms, one bathroom, and one kitchen. The whole house was probably about this size here. It wasn't a real big

[79] Shirley Hong Woo Kwan. "Growing Up in the Mississippi Delta," Unpublished, 2001.
[80] Frieda Quon, Interview, Jan. 12, 2000.
[81] John Paul Quon, Interview, Dec. 2, 1999.

house. I think back then that was just the thing you did. You lived behind the grocery store.[82]

So it was the living quarters that were attached to the store. What it amounted to was a block, it was a solid block. It was four storefronts. Two storefronts were the store. Then two storefronts were the bedroom, where our quarters were. We had five bedrooms and two baths back there. It was pretty comfortable. We had a buzzer. We were always a slave to that store. You would have one or two people out in the store... if it got busy, they would hit that buzzer, and we knew we had to take off and go (help).[83]

I played mostly when I was growing up before I started going to school. We had our store in the black area of town. We lived in the back of the store. I played mostly with the children around the store, which was great...I had a really hard time starting school. I had a good many good friends. Just went to school and came home. I never went to the games (high school sports). That was the main thing with the Chinese culture, is that you stayed at the store and worked for the parents.[84]

Oh yeah, they all helped (in the store)...They learned how to sell candy and coke ... when the were five or six years old they could make change for ten dollar bills. ... They learn to cut bologna. They learn how to chop neck bones with the cleaver. ... I remember the butcher would always put one of the boys (so) he would stand up in a chair. So he could get higher so he can weigh the meat. He could pack the meat for them. They would always help.[85]

---

[82] Bobby and Laura Jue, Interview, Feb. 4, 2000.

[83] Juanita Dong Interview, May 1, 2000.

[84] Penney Gong Interview, Oct.. 7, 1999.

[85] Bobby and Laura Jue, Interview, Feb. 4, 2000.

Figure 36 The Mee Jon grocery rearranged merchandise to seat guests for a birthday celebration dinner party. Courtesy, Delta State University Archives, Cleveland, Ms.

Children in those old country stores, you saw everything going on. We learned about life all through it. A lot of people brought the eggs and the country butter to sell to you to swap for something else. We had to pump kerosene. We even had a barrel of vinegar that we pumped. People would buy it by the quarts and gallon.[86]

I think we all started out making change. We used to have a little carpenter aprons (with pockets for coins to make change)...Each of us kids would be assigned to sell different items...One had the potato chips. One had the peanuts. One had the cokes. You made sure you collected (payment) what ever went out of your division. So we started doing that at a very early age. We all had our responsibilities just as did

---

[86] Lillie Woo, Interview, Feb. 14, 2000.

Fay's (her husband) family. I think all of us were raised the same way. Certain people were supposed to sweep. You had to fill up the drink machines. You had to stack groceries. You had to do all the things. There was always a lot to do as far as helping with other kids, of course, because our youngest sister is sixteen years younger than me...[87]

We even had to deliver groceries. In country towns you just have to do about everything. We all had to work. We couldn't stay and watch a ball game. My daddy would come pick us up. And give us a good whipping with those horse bands that you used to bridle the horses. It was really something as the years went by, we always tell my little sister and little brother that they were really fortunate they didn't have to do as much we. My sister and I were the oldest. Naturally all the work fell on us. One of us, well she did most of the baby-sitting of the younger children. I was in the store more than she was. [88]

Our lives revolved around the store; meals, studying, baths permitted according to the store's activities; when we were capable we had duties. With five children and five adults, children were assigned times to be in the store. A buzzer sounded when help was needed; we were slaves to that buzzer. Everything required service, customers could drive up, honk their horn for a soda pop, honk again to return the bottle. Meat was cut on request, grocery list could be phoned in, orders delivered by porters on bicycles and cold items were placed in the refrigerator. With long hours sometimes we fell asleep in the store waiting to close.[89]

My two sisters would also help in checking out the groceries, running the cashier stand. And then when I reached five, and they had (little) confidence (in me) of course, I could run up a

---

[87]Juanita Dong, Interview by Kimberly Lancaster, May 1, 2000, transcript, Delta State University Oral History Archives, Cleveland, Ms.

[88] Lillie Woo, Interview by Kimberly Lancaster and Jennifer Mitchell, Feb. 14, 2000, transcript, Delta State University Oral History Archives, Cleveland, Ms.

[89] Frieda Quon, Interview, Jan. 12, 2000.

cash register and things like that…but when they had confidence that I could make change, then they turned over the candy counter to me. We sold candy, ice cream, and soft drinks…There were like thirty-something different kinds of candy. I can remember they gave me a carpenter's apron because it was short. And I held my money in those pockets. And I would sell the goods and make change. And on one Saturday I sold $200 worth, and that's when a soft drink was (just) a nickel. [90]

As the oldest child, I helped cut expenses by doing many tasks in the store. The next oldest children could not do much to help in the store so they looked after five very young children in the home located a couple of steps from the store. A black servant cooked until the kids returned from school. Two young high school age black boys worked after school to stock shelves, bag groceries, and deliver customer orders on tri-bikes.

My father would be exhausted by evening from the long business hours each day because of his age, smoking … So by the time I was only 13, I sometimes had to run the whole store operation when my dad retired early in the evening. When problems arose that I could not resolve, I did have to awaken him for help. I opened and closed the store daily, managed and paid the black workers.

All the salesmen wanted to take advantage of my dad's absence by pushing their merchandise on me but I learned to make very sure that for every purchase order they got I also received rebates of some free goods. I trained new relatives to run their own stores, painted window advertisement signs, made weekly newspaper ads to print in the *Delta Democrat Times* every Wednesday, and dealt with customer relations. Every two weeks I had to place orders with M & H, a wholesaler located in Memphis, from whom we purchased groceries, frozen food, produce, and vegetables.

---

[90] John Paul Quon, Interview, Dec. 2, 1999.

> To run the store successfully, I also had to be a "Jack of all Trades" as an electrician, plumber, repairman, stocker, manual price stamper, cashier, meat cutter and packager, and salesman. I learned how to order daily produce.[91]

The successful operation of a store depended on the contributions and efforts of the entire family. Children processed requests from customers for merchandise, tallied their bill, accepted payment, and made change. The children of grocers had a far better command of the English language and grasp of American customs than their immigrant parents so they often had to help parents communicate with customers and serve as translators of written materials.

Dealing With Customers

During the Jim Crow era merchants throughout the South in businesses that involved serving customers typically conferred quicker, more courteous, and friendlier responses to white than to black customers. In line with this tradition of racial bias that prevailed in the South during those years, many Chinese grocers similarly gave more favorable attention to white than to black customers. A study conducted in 1966 used structured interviews of 50 non-Chinese familiar with Chinese grocers in several towns to assess their perceptions of how Chinese interacted with their customers and came to the following generalizations.[92]

---

[91] Robert Chow, e-mail to Author, March 27 and 28, 2008.

[92] Rummel, "Delta Chinese," 50-51. This Master's thesis had a non Chinese sample that was 20% merchants and 20% planters, with the other 60% including judges, doctors, ministers. Interviews measured their views about grocer relationships with their communities. The perceptions may have reflected experiences dating back a decade or more even though the research was collected in the mid 1960s.

The Chinese exhibit an attitude of condescension toward their Negro customers, while they exhibit an equalitarian attitude toward their white customers. However there are some variations introduced in all situations, and they need to be examined.

In the smaller towns, the Chinese grocery stores serve both white and Negro, and the attitudes that the Chinese have toward their customers is quite evident. The white customers are appreciated, and there is a great deal of interaction observed between the white customers and the Chinese grocery men. Generally, the interaction process is initiated by the Chinese, and then continued by the white customer. This is the case in many of the larger Chinese stores in the larger towns, but this relationship is the most evident in the smaller towns. This type of situation was observed whether the customers were male or female in the interaction process.

Relations with the Negro customer take on an entirely different approach. In both large and small towns, and in large and small stores, no matter what the location, a distinct air of condescension, and often indifference, is evident. The Negro customer is expected to enter the store, state the manner of his business, and leave. There is no process of interaction as there is with the white customers. There seems to be no particular desire on the part of either the Chinese or the Negro to participate in any sort of interaction process.

Of course, all Chinese grocers did not exhibit such preferential treatment, and the extent that any such bias reflected their personal feelings or was an unconscious conformity to the expected public conduct between races in a highly segregated society is unknown.

Good business practices call for merchants to be solicitous to customers, black or white, to retain their patronage. Chinese grocers with mostly black customers had good reason to treat them fairly as it would increase their competitive advantage over white grocery stores, which did not always welcome or rely on business from blacks. [93]

> ...We did make a living off of them (blacks), but we treated them with respect more than if they went to a Caucasian run store. We treated them with respect. We thanked them. We showed them that we appreciated it. We always spoke to them nicely. We never said any bad things to them. You can tell when you walk into a store, how the management will treat you right away. You can sense it. We always treated our customers with respect as a human. I think that is the reason why we do so well. I think that is the reason why Chinese in general did well.

Chinese grocers had subtle differences in communication styles with white and black customers. Obeying the unwritten rules of social etiquette embedded in the racial structure of the Delta, they respectfully greeted white, but not black, customers as Mister 'Smith,' or Missus 'Jones,' for example. Chinese did not address most white customers by their first names, but tolerated white customers greeting them by their first names. This arrangement created a sense of familiarity that made white customers feel at ease or even superior during conversations with Chinese who exhibited politeness bordering on the excessive.

During conversations with whites, to a greater extent than with blacks, a grocer might try to "accommodate" or go along with the views or opinions of the customer. Even if they disagreed with the speaker, as a matter of courtesy and way to avoid conflict, they would agreeably pretend to accept the customer's comments. Another method that showed deference to white customers entailed switching topics whenever

---

[93] Bobby and Laura Jue, Interview, Feb. 4, 2000.

conflicts seemed to arise. The grocer skillfully defused such encounters by deftly changing the topic of conversation to a less touchy one.[94]

Both deference tactics fit the values of Southern etiquette as well as those of Confucianism. Their use enabled the Chinese merchant to gain acceptance among whites by not posing a threat to them and all the while still maintain Chinese values. However, the use of these conversational tactics has weakened over time, especially for later generations of American-born Chinese in the Delta, many who now live in urban areas. They have higher education, professional careers, and expect more equitable treatment. They see no need to "defer" to others to maintain harmony and are more inclined to express how they really feel on a topic, albeit with some tactfulness.[95]

Chinese grocers, like other merchants, developed techniques to stimulate customer spending. For example, a grocer might give small gifts of food to the best customers at Christmas time to create good will.[96] Ted Shepherd, the long-time minister for the Chinese at the Baptist Church in Greenville described sales techniques that some Chinese grocers used with black customers to encourage purchases.

> When he (the black customer) comes to the checkout counter where he pays for that item, there in front of him are all kinds of candy and cookies. They are for a penny, nickel, and dime. The Chinese grocery man will give him his change, and he would look at his change and look at those items. He will pick him out some candy. The Chinese would take back some of the money, you see. they are very smart businessmen. The black man uses the Chinese store like you

---

[94] Robert Seto Quan, *Lotus Among the Magnolias.*
[95] Gwendolyn Gong. "The changing use of deference among the Mississippi Chinese." *English Today*, 19, (2003): 50-56.
[96] Bobby Joe Moon, e-mail to Author, Nov. 3, 2007.

use your refrigerator. The Chinese know that, and they make money out of the black neighborhood. They really do.[97] [98]

Shoplifting

Shoplifting was a concern for all merchants. Such thievery was more likely whenever the store was crowded as some customers saw it as an opportunity to get away with taking merchandise without payment. Grocers relied on vigilance as a deterrent, because once items were shoplifted, merchants had little recourse. It would have created bigger problems than it was worth to confront the culprits or try to press charges against them.

> Most of the time, we definitely saw them stealing, but we had no time to catch them. We had to make the cashier transactions as fast as possible so that the customers could eat soon. The things people stole were generally small but expensive, such as butter, fresh fruits (quite dear in those days), small cakes, soaps, spices, and so forth. Shoplifting was an art. A single person alone could do it. More often, it was done in pairs. One person pretended to buy something behind the counter. While the store clerk was reaching the merchandise with the back facing the two, in less than two seconds the other partner took the really intended items and ran out of the store.[99]

Grocery Robberies and Homicides

The small grocer was always an easy target for robbery. He had cash, worked late hours, and was in an area of poverty. Unfortunately,

---

[97] Ted Shepherd. *The Chinese of Greenville, Mississippi.* (Greenville, Ms.: Burford Brothers Printing Company, 1999)

[98] For more extensive examples of how Chinese merchants employ 'serial buying and selling' tactics with black customers, see Robert Seto Quan, *Lotus Among Magnolias, 30-32.*

[99] Zhou Liang, "Life of a Chinese American Grocer in the South"

over the years, a number of Chinese grocers were not only robbed but some were shot and even killed in their stores.[100]

> My brothers continue to operate Min Sang Grocery in spite
> of the risks. They have experienced hold-ups but were not
> harmed. The neighborhood park is now a hangout for drug
> dealers and drive-by shootings. In family run stores with
> only one or two persons, Chinese merchants become easy
> targets; there have been several cases of robbery and murder
> involving Chinese families. Even in the small town of
> Moorhead, our Chinese neighbor was murdered in broad day
> light for just a few dollars. I worry about the safety of my
> family but they insist on keeping the store.[101]

Ted Shepherd lamented the substantial risks to life and limb that Chinese grocers faced constantly from assault and robbery in their stores.

> I have buried three (that) I can think of, Chinese that were
> murdered in their stores. Mr. Pang had two or three narrow
> escapes. When I first went into mission I picked up the
> paper one night after supper to learn Pang's Grocery had
> been robbed. Lou and I immediately jumped up and got in
> the car and ran over there. We said, "We didn't know about
> this, Mr. Pang. Are you okay?" "Oh, that happened the
> other day. I am alright, alright." He begins to tell us about
> the robbery. He moved over in the center of the store and
> planted his feet. He said, "Now look down," and I looked
> down. He said, "See that bullet hole; that was the bullet hole
> the boy fired. I was just standing just like this."

> There is (sic) incidences where, for instance, a storekeeper
> named Pact Kee Kwan, had a store on the corner of Nelson
> and Broadway in the old Joe Gow Nue number two store.
> Two teenagers that were doped up came in and demanded his
> money. Evidently he knew them. There were just young

[100] As recently as in 2007, a 16 year-old robber shot and killed a grocer and his clerk in their store one night. "Grocer, employee shot to death in Shaw armed robbery." *Associated Press*, Sept. 20, 2007.
[101] Frieda Quon Interview, Jan. 12, 2000.

teens. Evidently he refused, and they shot him. I had to go back with a family member after that to get his personal effects from under the cash register. I saw that floor spattered with blood. Ironically I saw a Bible that I have given to Pact Kee with a gospel tract in it just above his head, and it was spattered with blood.

I want to say this ... in the Mississippi Delta, in Greenville particularly, every day a Chinese storekeeper gets up and enters his store he puts his life on the line. That is a strong statement. We'll have you know there is a high prevalence of drugs in our community. When a person wants drug money, and they don't have it, they think immediately that Chinese stores have money, and they target Chinese stores. This, we are talking about 1999... but it wasn't happening when I first started. There was some robbery, but it wasn't as bad as it is in these later years. So yes, we have had some bad experiences like that. Sorry to say, they happen. I think every Chinese store has experienced robbery. They have experienced robbery either with knifepoint, club, pistol, or a shotgun. I have seen shotgun blasts up on the wall, a hole that big ...bullet holes were in the floor.[102]

The Decline of Chinese Grocery Stores

The vast need for labor to handpick cotton shrank drastically by the 1950s when reliable harvesting machinery became available (earlier cotton-harvesting machinery often shredded the cotton fibers). As the mechanization of cotton picking increased, combined with the rapid decline of cotton prices, the grocery stores suffered a reduced income because of the smaller black work force.

As unemployment became more widespread, welfare became more prominent as a way of life. Many customers survived off food

---

[102] Ted Shepherd, *The Chinese of Greenville.*

stamps, which did not hurt the grocery business, but reduced the incentives of their customers to work.

> Well, by that time… they had food stamps. They had more money to spend than they would get with working. Like I said, by that time some of the merchants that were here earlier started to modernize the store a little bit. It is not so much as a service thing, but a self-service thing. You just pick your own groceries and things. At that time most of the people were called day labor. They worked in the field for so many dollars a day… They would operate a tractor for so many dollars a day. Right after, probably in the early fifties and late forties, Chinese started the process of changing their stores over to self-service. As far as scanning and things, we were out of that business by the time that it got to all of that.[103]

The Chinese grocers were faced with a need to modernize their stores at the same time when economic prospects for the region were declining. Adding to their difficulty, the massive social changes brought by the civil rights movement during the 1960s adversely affected the social and economic conditions for running Chinese grocery stores.

Robert Chow remembered the significant impact these social reforms in the Delta had on the fate of the grocery business of his adoptive father, Lucky Chow.

> When Lucky Food Store No.1 first opened in 1955 on the east side of Kentucky and Alexander Street, it was a white neighborhood. Few blacks were around our store area as this part of Greenville was then outside the city limit where the property was more expensive.
>
> After the Civil Rights Act came about 1964, blacks exerted more influence in voting and acquired more wealth. Some

---

[103] Juanita Dong, Interview, May 1, 2000.

bought homes in the white neighborhood, which started the white flight and the beginning change in Greenville demographics. Demographic change in Greenville affected the small grocery businesses for the Chinese when the whites moved away to avoid the black encroachment into their neighborhood. When one white family sold their home to a black, the whites began to move out toward the city outskirt. I believe the Civil Right Acts began to change Greenville real estate and led to the flight of the middle class white, which also hurt our business. Once it was a thriving business with both black and white customers, but it became a mainly poor black business. In a few years it changed to selling carryout, serving homemade fried chicken with some small grocery items.

Many Chinese I saw were just making ends meet struggling in their tiny corner grocery stores. Joe Gow Nue and Lucky Food Store #1 and #2, and Bing's Food Store were the biggest but the town (Greenville) was not big enough to support all of them with the vicious competition from the white mega stores.[104]

Thus, supermarkets with their large sales volume could offer much lower prices than the Chinese could match, which took away much of their business.

For example, many of the items heavily advertised by the supermarkets were selling for less than the wholesale prices that the small grocery stores paid. On the other hand, supermarkets offered no credits, all were owned and operated by whites, and were too far from the neighborhoods of the blacks who had no cars to go to distant stores. So, the Chinese-operated stores could still survive. But the volume of business and profits certainly were not as good as that during wartime. When the economy became depressed, the blacks would be the first to be laid off. Whenever there was

---

[104] Robert Chow, e-mail to Author, March 28, 2008.

layoff or labor strike, the grocery business suffered. Also, when the harvest of cotton had a bad year.[105]

A similar view was expressed by a grocer, Mr. Tong Mein:

...business is tough these days for small stores like mine. It's not what it used to be back in my father's days. Then there was nobody but Chinese in the grocery business. Little by little the chain stores, supermarkets like Sunflower and Kroger, came along and took over. You see, their prices are better, and they deal in volume. Plus they have their own brands, and they can afford to sell cheaper than the Chinese.[106]

Some small stores soon closed as their owners were not able to afford the expense of changes needed to compete with the large white-owned supermarket chain stores. Some of them were ready to retire anyway, and these conditions coupled with the lack of interest among their college-educated children to carry on their businesses, hastened their decision to sell or close their stores.

Despite many arduous aspects of the grocery store life, there were also positive aspects for Chinese families. For example, although many stores were located in impoverished neighborhoods and the physical living space in back of the store was typically crowded with few, if any, amenities, children did not seem to be any the worse for wear. Not having had prior experience with luxury, they did not suffer from their austere physical living conditions. Many lived and grew up playing with children of other races, without undue conflict. More important for their

---

[105] Zhou Liang, "Life of a Chinese American Grocer in the South"

[106] Robert Quan Seto, *Lotus Among the Magnolias*, 76.

psychological well-being was the sense of feeling secure, loved, and cared for by parents concerned about their futures.

Looking back on her family life growing up in their store, Frieda Quon remembered many positive aspects of the neighborhood around their grocery store in Greenville during the 1940's.

> Growing up in the 40's and 50's, life was so much simpler, we felt completely safe, no need to lock your car – a sharp contrast from today. With five children, my mother got a maid who supervised us seven days a week. My siblings (two brothers and two sisters) played at the white neighborhood park, only a block from the store. Mainly we played with each other; sometimes we played with the white children; I don't recall being ostracized or anyone mistreating us; besides Fannie, the maid was our protector. Occasionally we even played with the black children who lived near the store. Children are generally not race conscious and will play well together just fine.[107]

In describing the relationship working in a grocery store side by side with her children as they grew up, Frances Wong reflected on the value of this experience:

> A papa and mama store is wonderful. You can have your children with you. Then when we closed up, we gathered at the table. We all shared the food together. The father will tell each of its children what to do and what not to do. We will have the family time. So it was wonderful that we had that store. We made an agreement. If he wanted to go fishing, hunting, or to California to see his people, I would stay at the store with my children to work, take care of the store. If I wanted to travel to a different part of the country or overseas, he and the children will take care of the business.

---

[107] Frieda Quon, Interview, Jan. 12, 2000.

> My oldest daughter would do the checking for the customers at the cash register. My second daughter and him would take care of the butcher shop. My youngest daughter would take care of stocking the groceries on the shelf. My girls each one helped in the store. At one time all four attended Delta State. Then all three girls got their masters at Delta State at one time. They helped in the store. That is what we gave them __ an education.[108]

Working together everyday in the store, parents knew where their children were and could monitor their activities. The children acquired discipline and responsibility by doing their share of work, which contributed to the financial success of the store, and they observed how hard their parents had to work. In the process, family members formed strong bonds to each other that endured over their lives. The grocery store experience proved to be a veritable school for learning about life in which children acquired attitudes, habits, and values that led to much success in school and in their future careers.

---

[108] Frances Wong, Interview by Kimberly Lancaster and Jennifer Mitchell, Jan. 19, 2000, transcript, Delta State University Oral History Archives, Cleveland, Ms.

6. School and Church Connections

They stand before God in equality with white children on Sunday, but on Monday they cannot stand before the same blackboard. David L. Cohn [109]

A long-standing Mississippi tradition of segregated public schools instituted in 1890 held that "separate schools shall be maintained for children of the white and colored races." However, it was not until the 1920s that this policy became an issue for the Chinese simply because there were few Chinese women in the Delta, with the 1920 census identifying only 6 adult Chinese females. Not surprisingly, then, schooling for Chinese children was not yet a problem.

When Chinese grocers began to bring Chinese wives and children in larger numbers, either from China or other parts of the U. S. around the 1920s, families began to grow and the problem of where Chinese children could go to school became a real concern. Although the policy of separate schools did not specifically mention Chinese or other Asian groups, authorities interpreted the law to mean that the Chinese children had to be excluded from whites-only schools because they were "non-white."

Another concern, not officially expressed, was that some of the early Chinese men fathered children with black women. White society, as well as the Chinese community, regarded these children as partially black and, on that basis, excluded from white schools. Otherwise, if all children from Chinese families were admitted to white schools, and some had

---

[109] David L. Cohn. *Where I Was Born and Raised.* University of Notre Dame Press: (Notre Dame and London, 1948): 157.

mixed racial background, they would in effect be violating the tradition of segregated schools. As one observer noted in 1935:

> There are many Chinese in the Delta. They are successful merchants. Some of them live with their Chinese wives; others have Negro mistresses and families of half-breed children. To the casual eye these children are often indistinguishable from full-blooded Chinese. The fear arose in the white community that if Chinese children were permitted to attend the public schools these Chinese-Negro half-breeds would go along. The result was separate schools for the Chinese, at the expense of the community, provided for by law. Theoretically these schools are of the same quality as the white schools. Actually it is impossible to make them of the same quality without prohibitive expense. Chinese children, therefore, do not enjoy the same for education that are open to white children.[110]

During the latter part of the 1920s, however, matters would change as Chinese in the Delta developed educational resources for their children through their increased participation in white churches. Thus, it was in Rosedale in 1924 that the local school officials notified Gong Lum, a respected Chinese grocer in town for many years, that his daughter, Margaret, could not attend a white school. This decision was made with some ambivalence because the Lum family had achieved good standing in the community.

In the fall of 1924, Gong Lum, sued in court to get his daughter, admitted to a white school.[111] The state attorney general affirmed the ban in 1927, and the Mississippi Supreme Court ruled against an appeal. The

---

[110] Cohen, Ibid, 156-157.

[111] This important challenge was completely ignored in a recent history of Mississippi school segregation. Charles C Bolton. *The Hardest Deal of All: The Battle over School Integration in Mississippi, 1870-1980*. (Jackson, Ms.: University Press of Mississippi, 2005)

ruling against Lum was based on the 1890 Mississippi Constitution. The court felt that yellow, after all, was a "color" so the Chinese were excluded from white schools. Undaunted, Lum appealed to the U. S. Supreme Court, but again the effort was rejected as shown in Figure 37. In frustration, the Lums moved to Arkansas where Chinese were not barred from white schools.[112]

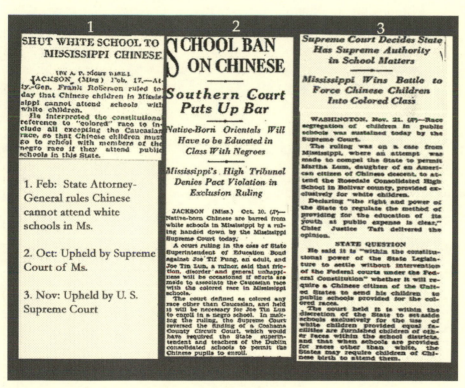

Figure 37 Mississippi attorney general ruling bars Chinese from White schools, and it is upheld by state and federal Supreme Courts in 1927. (1) Shut White School to Mississippi Chinese" Los Angeles Times, Feb. 19, 1927 (2) "School ban on Chinese" Los Angeles Times, Oct. 11, 1927, 1; (3)"Supreme Court Decides State has Supreme Authority in School Matters" New York Times, Nov. 22, 1927, 14.

---

[112] Jeannie Rhee. "In Black and White: Chinese in the Mississippi Delta." *Journal of Supreme Court History: Yearbook of the Supreme Court Historical Society* (1994): 117-132.

Chinese placed a high priority on education as the way for their children to improve their station in life. In the words of one Chinese, Audrey Sidney:

> What conditions did they encounter? They worked hard, and one thing they instilled in their children was to get a good education. An education was one of the highest priorities for us when we were growing up. Back then [many] Chinese people did not believe in girls getting a college education because they believed girls would get married and raise children. My parents believed that girls should be educated. Sometimes some of their friends would ask our parents, why are you sending those girls to college and comment that they don't need to go to college.[113]

In view of the school decision that relegated Chinese children to the inferior quality black schools, some Chinese grocers decided to send their children back to China to get a Chinese education. For example, Frances Wong of Louise, and her siblings went to school in China for several years until 1937 when war with Japan was imminent when they hurriedly returned to the Delta. Sam Sue of Clarksdale also went to school in China for several years. Lee Hong's grandfather sent 10 children back to China for a few years for the same reasons.

Other Chinese elected to find other states that allowed Chinese to attend white schools. Sue-Ling Wong vividly recalled being sent to Memphis for schooling:

> Our education was so very important to my parents. They always spoke of how it was the way for us to become more accepted and succeed in America ...It was in the summer of

---

[113]Audrey Sidney, Interview by Kimberly Lancaster, Feb. 4, 2000, transcript, Delta State University Oral History Archives, Cleveland, Ms.

1939 when my daddy finally decided it was time to send the three of us to Memphis to stay with our relatives for our high school education. We had never seen a school so big before, there were three gyms, a pool and two floors ... it was like out of the pages of one of our literature books. Anyway, it offered so many classes and I know I learned a lot there...more than I would have ever in Cleveland.[114]

Despite the legal ruling, in practice, enforcement of the barrier against Chinese attending white schools varied across communities. Instances where there were no objections typically involved small towns with only one or a few Chinese children. This ruling against the Lums notwithstanding, if you had good friends with the influential white leaders in town, they would not prevent Chinese children from going to their schools.

Problems arose for Chinese attending white schools only if someone in the town objected, which was a rare event if the family was well liked. However, in many towns the race barrier against the Chinese and blacks stood firm until 1970 even though the civil rights movement started earlier in the 1950s.

The Church Opens The Door To The School

In 1928 the Baptist Church in Rosedale, followed soon by churches in other towns such as Cleveland and Greenville in the early 1930s, decided to reach out and provide the Chinese with classroom instruction denied to them in white schools.

---

[114] Quoted in Sieglinde Lim de Sánchez, "Crafting a Delta Chinese: Education and acculturation in twentieth-century southern Baptist mission schools." *History of Education Quarterly,* 43, 1, (2003): 74-90.

This was a golden opportunity, both for the Baptist mission effort to attract Chinese to join the churches and for the Chinese to receive better quality schooling. Both parties recognized the benefits of such an arrangement that enabled Chinese children in and near these two large towns to attend the primary grades at the Baptist church even though they were still excluded from state supported white public schools.[115]

Greenville Mission School

Mrs. Galla Paxton, President of the Women's Mission Union in Greenville instigated a move to offer school instruction to Chinese children at the First Baptist Church in 1934. First, it was necessary to attract the Chinese grocers to participate in church services so that they would be interested in having their children attend church schools.

The initial problem was how to attract the Chinese who understandably were suspicious of initial overtures. A path had to be created to reach them. In Greenville, for example, the Women's Mission Union approached the Chinese with informal social calls in their stores with the aid of respected community leaders such like Joe Ting, which eventually convinced some Chinese to come to Sunday afternoon services held in Chinese. Pickup transportation and special church services at 2:00 on Sunday were arranged to accommodate the grocery family's work schedule. The decision to hold separate services for the Chinese and whites was not based on racial discrimination. The limited ability of many Chinese to understand English dictated that separate language services be

---

[115] John Thornell. "Where East meets West at the foot of the cross: The Chinese mission church in Greenville, Mississippi." Paper presented at *Southeast Conference of the Association of Asian Studies*, Jekyll Island, Georgia (2003).

offered. Neither the Chinese nor some members of the white congregation felt comfortable attending the same services because of their unfamiliarity with each other in this context.

Figure 38 The one-room Oriental School near the levee in Greenville, Ms. Courtesy of Ted Shepherd.

By the time Chinese were finally admitted into white schools, Shirley Hong Woo Kwan of Greenville had been attending the Oriental school for four years. She recalled that:

> It was called the Oriental School because all the students were Chinese. The Greenville Public School system back then was for Colored and White. The Chinese were considered neither. There were about thirty to forty students from grammar school through high school. Each class was small. There were only three girls in my class.

> The desks in the Oriental School were screwed into the wooden floor. The seat part had the front part of the next desk. These were the kind of desk you could not budge. There was a hole on the right side of the top of the desk. This held the ink well (ball point pens were not invented then). Also there was a space (groove) to put your pencil

so it would not roll. A section was underneath the desk to put your books.

In the building, there was one restroom. The sink was installed outside the restroom so everyone could wash their hands when needed. There were several windows to let some sunlight into the room. A teacher's desk and chair was up front, as well as a chalkboard, chalk and other necessary school supplies and equipment needed for teaching.

Although segregated, since we were considered part of the public school, a Caucasian teacher was provided to teach us. Because there weren't too many students in each grade, the teacher got to make her daily rounds to each grade level. [116]

Figure 39 Students in the Oriental School, Greenville, Courtesy, Delta State University Archives, Cleveland, Ms.

Cleveland Mission School.

Around 1934 Reverend Ira Eavenson, who had previously done missionary work in China led efforts to provide about 150 Chinese children with better education through the establishment of a Chinese

---

[116] Shirley Hong Woo Kwan, "Growing Up in the Mississippi Delta."

Mission School in Cleveland (See Figure 40). Chinese merchants from Cleveland and Boyle canvassed the region to gain contributions for the school with the aid of Rev. S. Y. Lee, the only native Chinese preacher in the state.

Community leaders from Boyle, Cleveland, Ruleville, Merigold, Duncan, Rosedale, and Greenville including Henry Joe, Joe On, Sing Gong, J. W. Sang, J. N. Wun, Joe Bowman, Joe Tong Im, Louis Joe, and J. H. Lett helped raise funds from grocers throughout the region to pay for the school facilities.[117]

In early 1937, the First Baptist Church, working with local civic clubs, the county, and the Mississippi Baptist Convention completed the construction of the school and a dormitory to provide room and board for those coming from distant areas during the school year. Chinese sent children there from all over the region. Two white teachers, Mrs. McCain and Mrs. Miller, paid by the county gave instruction in the curriculum of white schools in English from 8 to noon while Chinese teachers provided Chinese lessons from 1 to 5 in the afternoon.

Margaret S. Miller, one of the white teachers in Cleveland gave this account of the early days of the school and how difficult it was to get it funded and operational:

> No, there was a small school in Greenville for the kids there. They probably just had one teacher in Merigold. We taught the whole deal. We taught first grade through the twelfth ... You know we had a pretty good little library where the state had donated some books. It must have been a hundred or so books. We may have had that second year, forty-five or fifty

---

[117] Peter Y. Joe, "The Joe Family of Boyle, Mississippi." Unpublished, (2007): 18-19.

students come in.

So they had some trouble with some of the teachers because they didn't understand Chinese very well. They didn't understand the children and their culture. So they thought that Mickey and I would understand them a little bit better because both of us had worked with them. He had worked with them for four years in the mission, and I had worked two years. It was quite an experience. If they understand Chinese real well, you didn't have much trouble getting the English over. We had some that came from South China, and it was a different dialect from what these spoke.

Dorms: they had a matron. One of the Chinese men lived there as well. Then there was an English lady there. She was related to Ms. Eleanor. The one that played the organ at the First Baptist church for so many years. She was matron for couple of years, and then they got somebody else, a Chinese person.

I think, I read or heard somewhere, that was the only Chinese boarding school either in Mississippi or in the South. The one in Greenville was not a boarding school. The children in this Chinese School here collected more money per capital for saving bonds during the war than in any place in Mississippi. When they were collecting cans and scrap iron and everything, they didn't ask the Chinese to help. Well the big Chinese boys were highly insulted. They wanted to know why they couldn't collect scrap. Well the situation, being what it was. I talked to Mr. Ramsey, the superintendent of education. He said, "why don't they collect out there in that neighborhood?" Of course that was in an area that might not have been good either. They took their cars. You see, gas was rationed. They just said that we just want go anywhere else. We will keep it here. We will just pile in one car and come to school. We had them coming from Duncan and Merigold. Now there were children there from Rosedale that boarded there. There were some from Arkansas and Marks, some from Drew and Ruleville. [118]

The fact that Chinese had white teachers, but were excluded from white schools, was indicative of the caste status that the Chinese occupied in Delta society. The language, curriculum, and textbooks in the church school facilitated the assimilation process, while the reality of segregation did not. The Chinese desire that their children also receive lessons in the Chinese language and customs also countered assimilation by fostering in-group loyalties and ethnic awareness and pride.[119]

However, the church schools were not accredited, creating a problem for Chinese children wanting to attend college. Consequently, some parents sent their children to out-of-state public schools, in California and Texas especially, for the last years of their secondary schooling.[120] These factors reduced the enrollment in the church-related schools provided for Chinese. By the early 1940s, having served their purposes, the enrollments at the church schools began to decline as the Chinese entered white schools, and before long they closed entirely.

---

[118] Martha S. Miller, Interview by Molly Shaman, Dec. 3, 1999. transcript, Delta State University Oral History Archives, Cleveland, Ms.
[119] Robert W. O'Brien, "Status of Chinese."
[120] Sieglinde Lim de Sánchez, "Crafting a Delta Chinese Education."

Figure 40 Cleveland Chinese Mission, First Baptist Church. Courtesy, Sung Gay Chow.

After World War II Chinese were better accepted in the Delta. In part, the recognition that China was an ally in the fight against Japan improved public attitudes toward Chinese. Moreover, respect for the Chinese increased because many young Chinese men from the Delta, some born in China, patriotically served in the war. Finally, Chinese benefited from more tolerant racial attitudes that blacks and whites in military service gained from their contact with the world outside the Delta.

> I think it changed the attitude of a lot of people…A war is bad, but after the Second World War a lot of people came back, and they accepted a lot more. They accepted a lot more of the different (people).   They accepted Chinese a lot more.[121]

After the war, Chinese children were allowed to attend the white schools in some areas by 1946, but it was not widespread until after 1950.

---

[121] Edward and Annette Joe, Interview, May 1, 2000.

One example of how decision-making on this issue was sometimes left to local sentiment occurred in Boyle .

> Around early 1946, my oldest brother Jim Fong inquired with the Boyle school board about allowing his brothers to attend the public school system. He had returned from the armed service after spending 3 years in the US army. He confronted the board members about letting his brothers attend public school since he had served his country during WW II. It happened also that one of the board members was Senator W. B. Alexander, who was a close friend of the family and lived in Boyle. Through his influence, my brothers and I were allowed to attend public school in Boyle in the fall of 1946.[122]

The Chinese children proved themselves highly capable academically. They were highly respected, and even envied, by whites for their educational achievements and aspirations. The words of one white teacher were typical of these views.

> I wish that all my students were as good as the Chinese. We've never had any discipline problems, and they have almost perfect attendance both at school and also at school functions... The parents are very cooperative in working for the school, and we never have any trouble getting Chinese mothers to serve as room mothers or working for the P. T. A. ...The Chinese ladies are always willing to serve as chaperones to school groups...They are workers in every respect. They work very quietly and don't try to run the whole school like other women do. They and their husbands will do anything, particularly if one of their children is involved...But this is not true just at school. The women work in the church missionary societies, and for the Red Cross blood drives, and anything that they are asked to help with. They don't go out and volunteer, but when asked to work they never hesitate. They have a sort of reserve that they never let down, but they

---

[122] Peter Joe. "The Joe Family of Boyle, Mississippi."

are still a very warm people...They know they need an education, and they do everything to get it. They respect educated people and always try to associate with them. Mind, they aren't all serious...they do get out and have fun when there is a time for having fun, but when they work they work. Often I think that many of our children could learn something from them.[123]

School Desegregation

The civil rights movement of the late 1950s forced the integration of public schools in an attempt to correct inequity of the separate but definitely *unequal* schools for blacks and whites. The quality of the black schools had always been much lower, as they received only about one tenth the amount of funding provided to white schools, which was itself among the lowest in the nation. Although segregated schools were outlawed by the U. S. Supreme Court decision in 1954, white segregationists formed Citizens' Councils to resist and delay the change. It was not until over 15 years later during the 1969-70 school year that Mississippi public schools were finally integrated.

However, the legal ruling against segregated schools was readily circumvented in the Delta as throughout the South. Many whites as well as Chinese, worried that integrated schools would be of poorer quality, moved their children to private schools and academies, which most blacks could not afford because of the high tuition. Between 1969 and 2002, public school enrollment plummeted, with only about half the previous number of students.

The School Opens The Door To The Church

---

[123] Rummel, "Delta Chinese," 58-59.

Most of the Chinese immigrants to the Delta from Guangdong, like Chinese in other parts of the world, were not Christians initially. In fact, most of the immigrants came from farming villages and had weak religious involvement of any sort back in China. They followed the moral and family values advocated by Confucius, but that was not a religion as much as it was a philosophy of moral conduct. It did not involve teachings about a deity or an afterlife.

The history of Christianity in China provides a background for understanding the difficult situation faced by white churches trying to reach out to the Chinese grocers in the Delta. Western nations had tried since the 17th century, without great success, to introduce Christianity to China.[124] China resisted missionaries because they were suspected of being instruments of imperialism and colonialism and banned it for over a century from 1724 to 1860 before evangelical American Baptists began in the 1830s to recruit Overseas Chinese in Southeast Asia who used their familial networks in Hong Kong to promote the spread of Christianity.[125] The Boxer rebellion and Taiping uprising in the early 1900s drove many missionaries out of China. Half a century later, the Communist regime that came to power in 1949 was a further blow to the efforts of missionaries to convert Chinese to Christianity.

Many missionaries returning to the Delta by the 1930s realized that there was a population of non Christian Chinese right under their

[124] John King Fairbanks, ed. *The Missionary Enterprise in China and America.* (Cambridge, MA; Harvard University Press, 1974).

[125] Joseph Tse-Hei Lee. "The Overseas Chinese networks and early Baptist missionary Movement across the South China sea." *Historian,* 63 (Summer 2001): 753–768.

noses that they could approach with their message. White church leaders felt a moral commitment to convert Chinese to Christianity. They believed the teachings of Christianity could offer peace and salvation to the Chinese grocers who may have felt loneliness and despair in a foreign country.

It was true that Delta Chinese did not have sufficient resources or population size for ethnic affiliations such as clan-based associations or tongs (secret societies) that Chinese had in the ethnic enclaves of larger west and east coast cities. But Chinese in the rural Delta did not need formal organizations to provide social contact. Most Chinese knew all of the other Chinese in their communities and nearby towns and socialized with them regularly on weekends.

A more compelling reason for the Delta Chinese to accept the overtures of Christian churches to attend was that participation could help pave the way for Chinese to become better accepted by white organizations. In the highly segregated Delta society, the Chinese realized that the Church offered a door through which they might gain better access to a higher social standing. The churches, in their quest to fulfill their evangelical mission, saw a golden opportunity to reach out to these foreigners in their midst and bring them to accept Christianity. Everyone had something important to gain.

Unlike white schools, which denied entry to Chinese until after mid-century, white churches began to welcome Chinese to attend services of worship in the early 1930s. The churches also provided English language classes to the grocers and schooling to their children. Adopting Christianity allowed the Chinese to gain better education for their children, greater white acceptance, and improved their standing in Delta society.[126]

This contact with the Chinese provided the Church with the opportunity to introduce Christian values and religious practices. In addition, Baptist women taught Southern cooking and household cleaning methods to Chinese women, with the hope that they in turn would socialize their children to southern white Baptist social values and religious beliefs and divert them from emphasizing Chinese language and cultural traditions.

Figure 41 Chinese Baptist Church, Cleveland, Ms. Courtesy of Peter Joe.

As one unnamed Chinese woman recalled about her experiences at the Church:

> ...we would spend most of the time reading from the Bible, learn how to eat with fork, knives, and spoons, and learn how to be good Baptists.... I don't recall them teaching much else, but it really helped us learn English and that made our parents happy. That way, when we came home, we could teach them the words we learned at school.[127]

[126] Sieglinde Lim de Sánchez, "Crafting a Delta Chinese Education."
[127] Ibid.

Christianity was palatable to the Chinese because it was congruent with Confucian principles, which stress families and moral integrity. Confucianism rested on the authority of the clan or extended family, and traditional values. Chinese immigrants wanted to instill Confucian principles like family values and respect in their children, who did not find Confucianism relevant in the United States. Christianity is also based on authority, although of a different type. It promised security and comfort to the Chinese immigrants living in cultural isolation in the Delta. Thus, immigrants could retain their traditional Confucian values and instill those values into their children even as they were being converted to the Christian faith.

Delta Chinese, especially in larger cities like Greenville and Cleveland, over time became highly involved with their participation in Christian denominations such as Baptist and Methodist churches. By one estimate, nation-wide only about 8 percent of Chinese participated or belonged to Christian churches while at least 25 percent of the Delta Chinese were church members and in Cleveland, Mississippi, over 50 percent belonged to a church.[128] Thus, the high level of church attendance among the Chinese reflected the traditionally strong presence and influence of the Christian church in the daily life of southern communities.

In 1941, a sociologist, made the following observation about how the white church shifted in its views of the status of Chinese.

Ten years ago Chinese were both members and communicants of the First (white) Baptist Church of

[128] S. W. Kung, "Chinese in American Life"

Cleveland, Mississippi. Today they are still members of the church, but they must attend special services. Sometimes the Chinese teacher will act in the role of teacher, and often the white pastor will conduct the service. As members of the church the Chinese are granted the right to use the First Baptist Church for weddings and other functions. At these affairs invited members of the white community may participate.

The religious contacts between members of the two groups, no longer being on a basis of complete equality, are indicative of a trend toward a more complete enforcement of the caste system upon the Chinese community.

Leaders of the Chinese community, although careful to be inarticulate on the matter of caste, do give indications of their feelings about being excluded from white schools. One informant wanted me to be sure to understand that the reason that the Chinese children were excluded from the Rosedale schools was that some of them were part Negro-an apt illustration of the informant's unwillingness to identify himself with the members of the other colored race.[129]

The conclusion was that by 1941 the Church viewed the Chinese as a lower caste. However, Chinese were pragmatic. They did not seem to object to this status, provided it meant that their children were no longer denied access to education. They knew they could not overcome the way Chinese were viewed by whites overnight. They felt that if their children could receive schooling comparable to that provided to whites their children could achieve a higher social standing.

Entering The Church Through The School

White Baptist churches took advantage of the segregationist policies that denied Chinese children access to white public schools by opening

---

[129] Robert W. O'Brien, "Status of Chinese."

schools that provided them with a better education than they could obtain in black public schools. Thus, at an early age, the church became a central part of their lives. In larger cities like Greenville and Clarksdale, for example, children of grocery families were regularly in attendance at Sunday schools and many of them, not surprisingly, readily embraced Christianity.

> Church became very important in our lives because the First Baptist Church was so persistent in involving the Chinese. As Chinese opened their stores seven days and were reluctant to close, the First Baptist Church offered a special Chinese service on Sundays at 2:30 PM, which continues today. My father George Seu and Great Uncle were charter members of the Chinese Mission in 1934. Attending church was automatic and an opportunity for Chinese to see each other. Other church activities involved children in Sunbeams, Girls Auxiliary and Boys Auxiliary, and Vacation Bible School in the summer. Through church and school our world expanded to learn about American customs. The Chinese women attended Women's Missionary Union, which broadened their view on Western culture when they visited the homes of the white church women. As Chinese families mainly lived in the back of their stores, visiting in these homes gave them insight on how American families lived and they experienced desserts – a new concept, as the Chinese diet seldom included sweets. From the onset there were so many who provided support and stepped forward when necessary to aid the Chinese. In Greenville, the Chinese came to rely on Rev. Ted Shepherd, longtime pastor of the Chinese Mission. A true friend of the Chinese, in times of emergency, the Chinese would call Brother Ted before calling 911. At the time I was growing up in Greenville during the 40s, 50s, and 60s regular attendance at the Chinese Mission would be over a hundred.[130]

---

[130] Frieda Quon Interview, Jan. 12, 2000.

At the time that I was growing up, there was a large Chinese population. My mother made sure that we went to church every Sunday. We had an elderly couple that came by and picked us up to go to church every Sunday. We also had Chinese church. We also had Chinese school in the summer. So we could make sure we learned about the Chinese culture, learn about the Chinese language, and still try to learn how to use it… the Chinese church played a very big role in trying to keep the Chinese community together… and to try to keep instilling their ideals. We were very fortunate to have a pastor that came named Dr. Jakem Chan. He was very educated and came with certain ideas about how he wanted to church to bring all the Chinese community together. He is the one who made us go to Chinese school during the summer months while we were off. That way we could learn the language., learn how to write it, and learn the Chinese culture and teachings. Also he wanted to make sure we were able to live within the American society with these same values.[131]

We don't go anywhere but to church. Anytime there was any party or gathering was in the church. We did not have all of that, you know what I am saying. We just go to church and have parties (there).[132]

Exactly how many Chinese were devoted Christians and how many just went through the motions to gain social advantages for themselves and their children is not easy to determine.[133] Certainly, in smaller towns especially, Chinese had fewer social reasons for attending Church. Some Chinese did not fully accept the beliefs of Christianity, but were willing to attend activities at the church to socialize or as a momentary escape from work.

---

[131] Penny Gong, Interview, Oct. 7, 1999.

[132] Frances Wong, Interview, Jan. 19, 2000.

[133] Based on my observations from interactions in 2007-8 with at least 25 Delta Chinese born in the 1940s and 1950s now living in Texas, California, and Mississippi, it is clear that their religious commitment is strong.

Well, we went to the Baptist Church. They came to the store to pick us up to go to church because our family wouldn't send us. When we got back from church we would work again. Otherwise that was the only free time we had. Someone would come and pick us up...if they didn't pick us up, we had to work.[134]

Robert Chow, of Greenville described his view of the role of religion among the Chinese there during the 1940s:

At age ten I was adopted to the Chow's family (in Greenville) from Hong Kong, where I was raised in a British missionary orphan home. I was taught more about the Bible (in Hong Kong) than what I learned in the South. In a larger city like Greenville, we were fortunate to have translator for the English sermon to Chinese. The Chinese were not allowed to mingle with the white church services and separate Chinese church services began at 2:00 afternoon. The majority Chinese businesses closed or were forced to close on Sundays by the blue Laws in the South.[135]

He felt that many Chinese families lacked deep religious conviction, judging by their absence from Church. He noticed however, that they went to weekly mah jong games anywhere they were available to be part of a social gathering. He thought the Church provided families with opportunities for social gatherings and receiving English language instruction. Even if some Chinese lacked religious conviction, he felt that attending church gave them a sense of whom God is.

As for me, true (religious) conviction did not set in until 1982 when my wife and I went to an independent Baptist church in San Ramon, Ca. to seek counsel. Even though I

---

[134] Mae Wing, Interview by Kimberly Lancaster. March 1, 2000, transcript, Delta State University Oral History Archives, Cleveland, Ms.
[135] Robert Chow, e-mail message to Author, March 21, 2008.

heard many Biblical stories from an early age in the orphanage, I did not fully understand the Bible until my marriage was in disarray. That is when we came to dedicate our lives to serve Him, as we totally understood what "saved" really meant.[136]

Even though Chinese attended church, it proved difficult to obtain donations from them and some pastors made home visits to encourage financial contributions to the church.

Tithing was not understood by many of the less devout Chinese church members. Chinese have the Confucian focus on the family already embedded from their culture so many Chinese believed this aspect of Christian religion was due to Western philosophy. Moreover, they hardly made enough hard earned money that they could "give it away." They must send money overseas for relatives, and foremost, they wanted to save money to send their children to college.[137]

An example that more clearly shows lack of religious conviction is provided in the testimony of one anonymous woman who confessed:

My daddy used to go there two or three times a week to learn English. He really didn't believe in Christianity…he would tell us so, but to fit into the Delta, you just have to be one. He always made us go to the Baptist Church so that we could have more advantages, and I guess it did help us younger generations in the Delta. I don't know of any Chinese who aren't Baptists from my generation__and strong ones at that.[138]

Sam Sue expressed another dissenting viewpoint about the impact of religion:

Our parents really forced us to go to church despite our vehement protestations. They weren't Christians themselves.

---

[136] Ibid.

[137] Ibid.

[138] Sieglinde Lim de Sánchez, "Crafting a Delta Chinese Education."

For us, the church gave no access to mainstream society; if anything we all saw church as being a total hypocrisy— teaching to love our neighbors as ourselves and then excluding blacks and others the next day. For perhaps my oldest brother Church was a refuge_ he wasn't permitted to attend a public school (since it was for either whites or blacks), so for the first years of elementary school, he was taught by ministers who had spent some time in China.

Chinese church sermons were delivered in Chinese--I recall sitting in the audience with my parents and being bored stiff since I didn't understand what was being said. Chinese church was more than a religious gathering--it was a time for the Chinese families to socialize.
You really can't generalize about the role of the church in our lives__there might be other families and children who used church as a means of access but for us it was as oppressive as the other cultural/social institutions that existed [139]

If spiritual salvation was not a sufficient incentive for church attendance, many Chinese would admit that public appearances at church on Sunday was important because attending church enhanced one's standing in the community, an outcome that was especially valuable for merchants.

Most of us businessmen belong to one kind of church or another. If you don't belong to a church, everyone around here wonders why. So many businessmen go to church to keep goodwill in the community. Some of those guys go the *Bok Guey Yea Thiu Hong* [white church] in order to mix with the *Bok Guey* [whites], look good, and get more business.[140]

The participation of Chinese merchants in church activities helped them gain the respect and acceptance by whites in the community. A

---

[139] Sam Sue, e-mail message to Author, Jan. 20, 2008.
[140] Robert Seto Quan. *Lotus Among the Magnolias*, 82.

small town minister commended the involvement of Chinese members of his church as follows:

> The Chinese are some of my most faithful members. Oh, they aren't here every time we open the door, but they are here when they should be; and they not only give their time, but their money as well. If you work with the Chinese, they work with you. They carry their part of the "load" and all the Chinese here in [Community] regularly attend services. The women seem to be particularly interested in the church work and they bring all their children just like the white ladies in the church do. The men don't come all the time because they often have their stores open on Sunday, but they come when they can. The Chinese are recognized here because they work for the church, and I feel that they get a lot out of it. [When this observer suggested that perhaps the Chinese are active in the church for business reasons, the minister ignored the question, but did say the following] To be a good church member the church has to have a good pastor and a good pastor will help direct his people in the right way, and the right way leads to success, no matter what one does. The Chinese couldn't have succeeded had they not been good church members, because the people here in [Community] don't trust somebody that doesn't go to church and pay his respects to the Lord. But these Chinese are sincere in all their worship just as they are in all other aspects of their lives.[141]

In conclusion, Chinese and the church enjoyed mutual benefits. The provision of quality educational opportunities in both the American and Chinese curriculum at the church school greatly benefited the Chinese who could not attend white schools. Not only did the children learn academic content, but they also began to climb the social ladder, which led them to expect and gain fairer treatment and respect from white society.

---

[141] Rummel, "Delta Chinese," 73.

Ironically, the resources of the Baptist schools also provided a means to help the Chinese achieve their own goals, which were quite different from those of the Baptist agenda. Specifically, Chinese wanted to instill Chinese language and culture in their children. For example, in Greenville, the First Baptist Church provided space and paid utilities for the Chinese school language, arts, and cultural instruction by Chinese teachers hired by the Chinese.

> The Chinese community wanted its children to take intensive history lessons on Chinese civilization in order to cultivate their knowledge and develop respect for their ancestral land. After the first two hours of lessons, they would then switch to other 'elective' art courses. [142]

By providing mission schools for their children, churches, especially of the Baptist denomination, were able to recruit participation of Chinese grocers in church activities, which eventually led many to embrace the Christian faith. And, by introducing young children to Sunday school, the church built a foundation for religious involvement among the succeeding generations of Chinese.

---

[142] Ted Shepherd. *The Chinese of Greenville.*

7. Segregation and Race Matters

Mississippi, like other states in the Deep South, had social institutions, customs, and practices favoring whites that had its roots in the slave origins of its black population. By the time the Chinese began to come to the Delta in the 1870s, white superiority was already a deeply rooted aspect of Southern society. Chinese were regarded as non-white and therefore, "colored." As they were not fluent in the English language and American values, they were also foreigners, and relegated to a low social status.

Race relations presented a delicate situation for the Chinese. They were economically dependent on the blacks that were the primary customers in most of their stores, but the Chinese wanted whites to accord them more favorable treatment than that given to blacks. In other words, Chinese had to walk along a thin line between the black and white segments of society. During the battle over school desegregation that arose in the 1960s, some Chinese hedged their bets, making private contributions to both the National Association for the Advancement of Colored People and the white segregationist Citizens' Councils. To be acceptable to whites, they had to distance themselves from blacks. But being economically dependent on blacks, as well as living in black neighborhoods, they had to treat blacks better than whites did.

The ambiguous social standing of the Chinese is aptly illustrated by the following observation about the opposing ways that Chinese were regarded by whites and blacks in their communities.

> We did have a problem with that (discrimination). In the
> community where we lived we were quite accepted, but the
> blacks considered us as whites. The whites considered us as
> non-black, but we were kind of stuck in the middle there.[143]

Race Attitudes Between Chinese and Black

Chinese Views of Blacks. The attitudes of the Chinese toward blacks
modeled the white dominance views that prevailed in Delta communities
during the days of Jim Crow laws. In the triangle of Delta races, Chinese
felt they had to distance themselves from blacks if they were to be better
accepted by whites. Moreover, Chinese values on education and
entrepreneurial achievements were more similar to those among whites
than with blacks.

However, within the Chinese community, there were strong status
differences based on interracial affiliations. Those Chinese with a greater
extent of social involvement with blacks were held in disfavor. In
particular, Chinese felt that sexual relations or marriage between any
Chinese and blacks harmed the standing or acceptance of Chinese among
Whites.

> In the early history of the Chinese in the Delta the Chinese
> males often had social relationships with Negro women, and
> these early relationships have led to a type of social
> stratification within the Chinese community. This is most
> evident in distinguishing the rich Chinese and the poor
> Chinese. The poor Chinese must associate socially with the
> Negro to a greater extent, and because the Negro is held in
> inferior status in the Delta any such associations bring
> disfavor to the whole Chinese community. Because of the
> desire of the wealthier Chinese to associate and to be
> identified with the white community, and because any social

---

[143] Penny Gong, Interview Oct. 7, 1999.

association by any Chinese with the Negro community is not one of the approved norms of the white community, such a stratification pattern has arisen in the Chinese community. [144]

One candid comment from someone who did not want to be identified by name recalled that:

> The Chinese looked down at blacks and saw them as low class, unintelligent. Just because blacks were the primary source of income for many Chinese grocers didn't mean that the Chinese and blacks liked each other. If anything the race relations were more akin to the relations that Korean green grocers had with blacks in the 1980's — usually antagonistic and poisonous relations. Blacks resented many Chinese but had little choice since no one else would open a store in their neighborhood.
>
> Our parents had a bit of a different experience. We had a store in the central business district whereas most stores were in the heart of the black areas. Most of our customers were sharecropping families and our parents knew them very well and on some level would call them friends. But in no way did our parents see blacks as equals.
>
> Curiously, our store was a bit of a melting pot—our store was a kind of saloon where you could have your beer or soda and eat sardines or lunchmeat. Blacks and whites (many rednecks) were all sitting around though not necessarily socializing with each other.

Although some Delta Chinese disfavored socializing with blacks, nonetheless they generally had harmonious relationships in business dealings with them.

> Black employees—general help, delivery boys, house maids — were treated well at our store. One incident I remember

---

[144] Rummel, "Delta Chinese," 88-89.

well. A white customer accused the delivery boy of driving recklessly when delivering groceries to his house. They must have had words. When the Chinese grocer got wind that the customer and his buddy was going to go after the delivery boy, he bought him a train ticket to leave town that very day. We never saw him again; Chicago or Detroit was his most likely destination.[145]

Robert Chow who lived in Greenville recognized that Chinese gave more deference to whites while treating blacks less favorably:

> Chinese has their own racial fault, more so about blacks. Chinese gave respect to the whites because they held sway in public offices and judicial position and because they have the wealth and power. The black was looked upon as poor, uneducated, and naive, always a servant and laborer and lazy by some Chinese. But to me, they were cordial, easy to get along, content, and helpful, hard worker. I had studied the U.S History, War Between the States, and Mississippi History. I still have many black friends in Mississippi and made many (black) friends when I was in the Air Force.[146]

Black Views of Chinese. Black prejudices against Chinese may have originated well before they arrived in large numbers in the Delta. Through black publications and newspapers, China of the mid 1800s was portrayed as ridden with poverty, famine, overpopulation, and civil strife. They conveyed an underlying resentment that stemmed from American missionaries making such great efforts in China to convert the Chinese while they ignored the plight of blacks in America. These negative views about the Chinese influenced their unfavorable attitudes about the

---

[145] Paul Wong, e-mail message to Author, March 5, 2008.

[146] Robert Chow, e-mail message to Author, March 21, 2008.

presence of Chinese immigrants in the Delta. Blacks formed views similar to those widely held by whites such as the belief that the Chinese, as foreigners, would never assimilate to western values and ways.[147]

On a more pragmatic level, the economic threat from Chinese cheap labor was perhaps the more immediate concern. In the 1870s whites felt Chinese were better workers who would not only be cheaper but also more reliable; hence, blacks resented Chinese as rivals. The potential loss of work created hostility of blacks toward Chinese in the Delta as in other parts of the South where Chinese laundries replaced many black washerwomen. However, as noted earlier Chinese in the Delta chose not to work the cotton fields, but opened grocery stores instead.

Black acceptance of Chinese improved because economic competition with them was minimal, and the presence of Chinese grocery stores in black neighborhoods was a convenient resource. In general, they also felt more welcomed in the Chinese stores than in those operated by whites. They also appreciated that some grocers extended credit to blacks and made donations to black churches. Still, blacks felt Chinese incorporated the negative attitudes of whites toward blacks, and consequently were prejudiced against them as reflected by white customers receiving better treatment.

Race Attitudes Between Chinese and Whites

Not only were Chinese blocked from attending white schools in Mississippi until the late 1940s, they did not have access to many other

---

[147]Arnold Shankman. "Black on yellow: Afro-Americans view Chinese-Americans." *Phylon*, 39, 1, (1978): 1-17.

white public facilities until after 1950. White hospitals would not treat Chinese patients, for example.

Shirley Kwan related that:

> Since the Chinese were not admitted to the White hospitals, my birth took place in the Hong's living quarters, a room located in the store named Fok Chung Grocery, which my parents operated ...I was delivered into this world by Dr. Jerome Hirsch, who was assisted by a Black lady named Lena Collins, who was a midwife ... In fact, six of Mom's seven children were delivered by them at home. One brother was born in the Colored Hospital on Broadway Street. [148]

This experience was just one of many she faced with white hospitals. When her brother suffered an asthma attack, he was denied admission to the white hospital. In 1968, when she gave birth to her third child, she did not even attempt to go the white hospital, but only two years later she was allowed to go to the white hospital for the birth of her fourth child in 1970.

Interestingly, although Chinese were not admitted into white hospitals for treatment, white doctors would attend them if they were seen in a hospital for Negroes.

> Some time ago a young American-born Chinese who is a leader of Greenville's Chinese colony, applied for admission to the King's Daughters' Hospital. Bent over with appendicitis pains, he was in need of emergency surgery. But he was denied admission. The institution does not take Chinese patients. It does take Chinese money donations. The father of the patient in question had once given it a contribution of five hundred dollars. The sick man then went to the Negro King's Daughters' Hospital. There _ such are the complexities of the color problem_ he was assigned a

---

[148] Shirley Hong Woo Kwan, "Growing Up in the Mississippi Delta." Unpublished.

private room so that he would not have to share quarters with a Negro. And there a white surgeon attended him.[149]

Matters were not always "black and white," as in cases of a Chinese married to a non-Chinese. The white wife of a Chinese went to a white hospital to give birth to her baby. In this instance, she, being white, was admitted, but the Chinese husband was not even allowed into the hospital to see his wife and newborn infant.[150]

Even though Chinese were able to attend white schools by the 1950s, they still faced blatant and often more subtle forms of racism in various forms from white school children ranging from fisticuffs to taunts and ostracism.

One respondent who preferred not to be named related how he and his brothers often faced verbal taunts from whites where they grew up and more than a few times got involved in fistfights with them. He recalled one vivid racist incident that occurred during a basketball contest:

> A white player on the opposing team spit in my face as I was moving down the court. When I told my coach what he had did, he (coach) told me to retaliate if he did it again. When the same player tried to spit on me again, I hit him in the face with my elbow and put him out of the game with a bloody nose. Needless to say, the player never did that again in future games that we played against them.

Gradually relationships with white students improved and they were treated more equitably by the time they were in high school as he and an older brother, both athletically skilled, were selected for the football, baseball, and basketball teams.

---

[149] David L. Cohen, "Where I was Born and Raised." 234
[150] Ibid.

By the 1950s, Chinese and whites generally got along in school but there was one area where racial mixing was frowned upon. When members of the opposite sex became romantically involved, negative reactions of both white and Chinese communities were prevalent in the 1950s and earlier in the Delta. White and Chinese parents felt that interracial dating and marriages were not viable, as illustrated by Robert Chow's reflections:[151]

> In my early teen years, just only handfuls of Chinese were in all-white schools. I never envisioned marrying any white girl but saw them only as friends. My adopted family constantly reminded me the hate letters and uproar created by one of their sons for even talking to one white girl in school in the 1950s; back then Chinese were not allowed with the white in public school. Whenever I attended school functions, teen dances, and graduation, I had to dance with a Chinese girl, but only two were available then. When I asked a white girl to dance, all eyes were on me, and it was not a comfortable feeling. Only I was daring enough to ask the white girl while my cousin waited out or skipped the graduation prom…I have to say many of the classmates had treated me well just as long as I don't cross the line with the white girl; I did respect it.

Even with the passage of many years and improved race relations between Chinese and whites, Robert was still adversely affected by his experiences when growing up:

> Since graduation, I did not make contact to any white classmate and only attended the class reunion twice. Nowadays anything goes, even my oldest son married to a white English girl but the pitfall came all too soon in their marriage. We had warned him on cultural barrier but to no avail. Interracial marriage can never be normal because there

---

[151] Robert Chow, e-mail message to Author, March 21, 2008.

is the cultural divide.

Similarly, Bobby Jue later recalled that he felt a sense of rejection from whites throughout his childhood in Hollandale. These experiences made him feel uncomfortable with whites at school. He always felt that some barrier existed between Chinese and whites, often subtle, and unspoken.[152]

Apart from physical features, which clearly distinguished Chinese from other races, many whites and blacks regarded Chinese as almost "white" because they were so assimilated into white culture and shared many of the norms and values of the dominant white group with respect to their economic, educational, and religious lives. In contrast, however, they showed limited assimilation in terms of informal social ties with whites, as reflected by their choice of friends, dates, and spouses.[153]

> Even though they have adopted the white norms and values, they still tend to put the greatest emphasis on their families and intimate primary group relations. They have their own interests and participate in white social functions in only a limited formal manner. The white community seems to accept the Chinese community more than the Chinese community accepts the white community. This social disassociation is evident in Chinese social organizations that are segregated against all but Chinese.

Whites attributed Chinese aloofness and reserve during social interactions with them as due to a self-imposed preference to stick with their own ethnicity for social relationships. While Chinese did prefer to socialize with other Chinese because of common culture and language,

---

[152] Bobby and Laura Jue, Interview, Feb. 4, 2000.
[153] Rummel, "Delta Chinese," 88.

they also felt that white racial prejudices against them left no choice but to maintain their social distance. From a white perspective, however, it was the Chinese who discriminated against whites rather than vice versa.

That Chinese were not confrontational in opposing discriminatory treatment and political passivity is seen as stemming from Chinese culture, although for young Chinese it probably reflects their unsure place in Delta society.[154]

> We have noted that young Chinese do not think or talk about their own cultural heritage. They also avoid discussing the social structure in which they live…Just as their parents are isolated by their racial position from active participation in Mississippi politics, so youth are isolated __ perhaps partly *by* their parents __ from political deliberations… the primary response of the young Chinese to their difficult position is to leave the state, and it is impossible to say they are wrong. They do not, after all, have the power to change it.

In part, these divergent views reflect Chinese cultural values of avoiding conflict and saving face. Moreover, the very small numbers of Chinese contributed to their stoical acceptance of their situation. They knew there was no realistic way they could win any direct confrontations against the perpetrators of racial intolerance when they were so vastly outnumbered.

Housing Restrictions Against Chinese

Chinese were not allowed to buy homes in white neighborhoods in many towns until after World War II. John Paul Quon remembered when his father tried to buy a house next to the Moorhead Baptist Church:

---

[154] Loewen, *The Mississippi Chinese*, 163-165.

And he had even made earnest money, placed earnest money for it and had basically closed the deal, until he got threatening letters. And the agent eventually brought in postal investigators, and they traced that letter back to a particular person.

However, John Paul's father had the last laugh in one transaction when he shrewdly outmaneuvered a white man who sold him a farm thinking that his father did not knew much about real estate dealings.

And, of course, it caused a shock within the community that here is a Chinese merchant buying a cotton farm. And the seller, I'm told by other members of the community that he was licking his chops. Because he turned around, and he took the down payment, and he held the note, thinking that my father would not be successful, and he'll get the farm back, and he'll pocket the down payment. Except at the end of the first year, my father made a decent crop, but he paid cash for the rest of the note. And it shocked the rest of the business community that my father had the cash… again, my father was prosperous. It was my mother that was frugal. She was the one that made sure that we didn't squander our money.

…my father then grew in stature because, again, you know, he'd bought the farm, and I'm going to use the word "outsmarted" the white community. And then built a house and was showing progress, prosperity. He brought three_no four_families over, and not only paying for their passage, but also even providing the capital for them to start a business. There's one_now that couple did sacrifice, but they did have capital from my father. They sacrificed so much that in the first month of their business they only ate sardines and crackers for the whole first month-you now, to build up capital so they can expand their business and what not.[155]

---

[155] John Paul Quon, Interview, Dec. 2, 1999.

Sam Sue's family also faced forceful resistance and opposition to their attempt to buy a house in a white neighborhood in the 1950s, which led them to abandon that effort in frustration.

> We tried to purchase a house in a white neighborhood (we had always lived in run down quarters in the back of the store) and the day before closing, we get a phone call that the house will be burned down if we buy it. Obviously the deal never went through. However the Chinese in the area banded together to boycott the Pepsi distributor, which was run by the person who had made the threatening phone call.[156]

Hiring Discrimination Against Chinese

Chinese saw improved white attitudes toward them after World War II. Many young Chinese American men from the Delta had served in the military, which earned the respect of whites. Many young Chinese focused improving themselves through education entered college and earned degrees. Still, there were obstacles that the Chinese faced. They still faced discrimination in many areas including access to many forms of employment. For example, in the 1950s several Chinese women reported being victims of school policies against hiring Chinese. Even though they had earned Mississippi State University and University of Mississippi college degrees, they still found that racial discrimination, often subtle rather than blatant, limited them to working in grocery stores.

Audrey Sidney related her personal encounter with blatant racial prejudice against hiring Chinese when she sought a teaching job in Greenville in 1956.

> I applied for a job at the Greenville Public School because that was where we were going to live. He (husband) had

---

[156] Sam Sue, e-mail message to Author, Jan. 20, 2008.

some job offers, but he decided to stay in Greenville and go into [the electronic] business with his brother. I applied for a job when I came to Greenville and asked for an interview. I had an interview with the superintendent [Greenville Public Schools], Mr. Koonce. He told me that only Caucasians could teach in the white public schools in Greenville. So he did not offer me a job. Of course, this was like a "slap in the face" to me, because I had not had that kind of treatment in growing up. Or maybe it would have good if I would have had that kind of treatment so it wouldn't hit so hard. I am the kind of person that always wanted to work. I enjoy working, I enjoy meeting people, and I enjoy doing something. Staying at home is not my life. I don't get joy out of cleaning, mopping floors, cleaning bathrooms, or doing the dishes. Anyway, so I couldn't get a job teaching in the public school, which was my major in college. I got a job at the Greenville Air Force Base. I worked out there in '57 and '58. [157]

Annette Joe described her similar encounter with racism in hiring when she applied for a teaching job in Jackson around 1957:

...That is the best paying place in Mississippi. I went over there. It happened that the superintendent of the schools was interviewing. I went in and said hello. He was nice enough.

Then he said, "Well I am sorry to tell you we just don't have anything at the schools at all." I said, "Sir I just came from an interview department. He said you have tons of vacancies. I said I think I am qualified. I had lots more. I went to Delta State every summer. My year was the first year that they were required a teacher's certificate. So I got a performance degree, which didn't include all of the psychology and all the biology and stuff that you have to take for the teacher's license. I took all of those things. I think that I am very qualified."

---

[157] Audrey Sidney, Interview, Feb. 4, 2000.

He said that it has nothing to do with your qualification.
Well, I want you to tell me why there is not a job. He said
well, we don't have a place for you. He said I am not ever
going to hire anybody like you. I said, "Well… how am I?"
He said, "Well, you are Chinese. I will never hire you to
teach in Jackson."[158]

Tri-Ethnic Relationships

Most discussions of race relations in the Delta examine races in
pairs such as black-white, Chinese-black, or Chinese-white. The analysis
of how Chinese dealt with blacks and whites when interacting with each
separately is valid in its own right but tells an incomplete story. Race
matters become much more complicated when considering the tri-ethnic
aspects of many Delta communities.[159] How Chinese behaved toward
blacks and whites was not based solely on their attitudes toward each of
these groups whenever members of all three groups were present. Thus,
if Chinese were too cordial toward blacks, their acceptance by whites
might be jeopardized. And since most of the Chinese grocers relied
heavily on black customers, they risked creating black resentment if they
fully embraced white attitudes and values. Chinese tried to strike a middle
ground as they had to convince whites that they were not too cozy with
blacks at the same time they had to persuade blacks that they did not
whole heartedly endorse white attitudes and values.

Social class and economic status was intertwined with race and
ethnicity in the Delta as whites, not blacks, held social power. Chinese
acceptance by whites was necessary for them to improve their social

---

[158] Edward and Annette Joe, Interview, May 1, 2000.

[159] "Tri-ethnic" community is a misleading label, as Chinese were less than a fraction of
1% of the population in most towns,

status, a goal that was achieved by distancing themselves from blacks except for business transactions. It was not the case that Chinese did not have prejudices against other races, black or white. However, these sentiments were accentuated in the highly segregated society of the time and place. To escape racial discrimination from whites, Chinese had to ignore, or even add to, prejudicial treatment that blacks suffered.[160] [161]

Chinese And Civil Rights Activism

The Chinese were in a precarious situation during the civil rights activism of the late 1950s and 1960s, often caught between the proverbial 'rock and hard place.' On one hand, they stood to benefit in the long run from better treatment of minorities. The older generation, long accustomed to passive acceptance and fatalistic views of their status in the Delta, did not participate in political activism. Being a very small minority, usually less than one tenth of one percent of the population, it was dangerous for the Chinese to get actively involved because they were caught between their black customers and the white power establishment, which often involved redneck and Klu Klux Klan elements. They feared repercussions and discouraged their young adult children from getting involved in social political activities.

---

[160] A documentary attempted to depict the bind faced by Delta Chinese by being caught between the black-white divide. It was not well received by Delta Chinese partly because they felt the film falsely portrayed them, focused on black-Chinese marriages, and ignored their achievements. Christine Choy, Worth Long, Allan Siegel. *Mississippi Triangle* New York: Third World Newsreel, 1984.

[161] Praised as an open-ended ethnography of race relations in a tri-ethnic society, it has also been criticized for ignoring social class. R. Bruce Brasell, "So that we have our own color: Mississippi Triangle, textual posturing, and racial negotiation" *Film Criticism, 2002.*

The intensity of racial tensions rapidly increased with each new development. In 1962, James Meredith was the first African American student to enroll at the University of Mississippi. His presence required the intervention of federal troops to restore order when violence broke out at the campus. Frieda Quon, then an Ole Miss undergraduate, vividly recalled the crisis, and described the reactions of the Chinese students:

> On the weekend he arrived, our peaceful campus became a war zone. National Guard troops were everywhere. As students we didn't know what we should do; we were scared to go anywhere. The American Chinese boys were in the dormitory facing the student union where much the action was; outsiders came on campus to protest, which resulted in tear gas being used for crowd control. It was pandemonium; John Quon took all of the Chinese girls home. After a few days we returned. Upon entering the campus, the National Guard required student identification and inspected the inside of our car and trunk for contraband. At the cafeteria only plastic utensils, dishes, cups were allowed. Meredith had to be escorted to classes with guards; he literally had to have protection 24/7. This event would change Ole Miss and Mississippi forever. [162]

The rampant uprising of blacks against segregation was often indiscriminate, and not limited to destruction of white businesses. Chinese grocery stores, located usually in black neighborhoods, also suffered from black violence in the wake of the civil disturbances of the 1960s. These actions led some older Chinese to sell their businesses, or retire, and move out of the Delta to avoid the dangers to life and limb.

As Penny Gong remembered:

> In Clarksdale the neighborhood where my parents had the store was still a quiet community. My parents had a good

---

[162] Frieda Quon, Interview, Jan.12, 2000.

relationship with the people we worked with, but during that time they (civil rights activists) were bringing people in from outside of Mississippi to try and stir up the movement.

Civil rights workers that came down may have gotten a bit carried away, but they burned my parents' store down thinking that they needed to get us. They thought we were white, and they wanted us out of the community there. The people that lived around my parents' store were devastated. My parents never rebuilt the store even though the people that lived around the store continuously called and wanting my parents to open the store back. It was too much. [163]

Because Chinese had improved their lot in the Delta over the years much more than blacks had, resentment by blacks toward Chinese was not surprising.

White grocers were always white. Chinese, however, were once in approximately the same position as blacks, were once brothers in oppression. Now, however, they have been allowed to join white institutions, move into white neighborhoods, and send their children to white schools, and they have lost no time in taking advantages of these opportunities…In addition, it is sadly ironic that the most visible result of the black liberation movement in the Delta has been the elevation of the Chinese to near-white status, leaving blacks more alone in their oppression. [164]

Although the Chinese did eventually benefit from the civil rights struggle, they were mainly passive spectators, partly because they were such a small minority. They also hesitated to be overtly involved, trapped between their sympathies with their oppressed black customers and their

---

[163] Penny Gong, Interview, Oct. 7, 1999.
[164] James Loewen. *The Mississippi Chinese*, 176.

fear of antagonizing powerful white organizations that could harm their businesses.

Racial Tolerance and Diversity

In a society with a long tradition of racial segregation, it is easy to overlook instances of racial harmony and acceptance. On the positive side, other whites that were more tolerant and accepting of Chinese circumvented some barriers facing Chinese by acting as intermediaries for them in buying homes in white areas.

Penny Gong described the situation her family faced with housing discrimination as late as the 1960s:

> In 1967, we tried to buy a house so that I could go to school at Clarksdale High School. We met much opposition. There was some people who were rather ugly to my parents, but those same people turned out to be some of our very best friends after we got to know them.
>
> ...Buddy Ellis was a judge in Clarksdale, and he was a very good friend of my father's. He bought our first house for us, and he signed the house over. He used my father's money to buy the house, and then he signed the house over to my father. After we moved in, our neighbors were just ignorant of the fact that we weren't different. [165]

Not all areas in the Delta were rigidly segregated by ethnic and race barriers. There were a few mixed ethnic neighborhoods where the residents enjoyed amiable and cordial relationships with each other. In many towns, most Chinese grocery stores were located in black neighborhoods where many of the playmates of their children, aside from

---

[165] Penny Gong, Interview, Oct. 7, 1999.

siblings, were black. In other towns, where their store was located in the white downtown business section, their playmates were more likely to be white children.

> I lived in a neighborhood where there was a mixture of cultures. There were Blacks, Whites, Jews, Lebanese, Irish, Mexicans, Native American, Indians, French, German, Italian and Chinese. My mom and dad ran the neighborhood store that fed all the people. Everyone got along, and we trusted and depended on each other.
>
> Since Dad could speak Spanish, he would converse with Ruby, the lady from Mexico. I remember the times that Mrs. Stockner, a Jewish lady, would always bring Mom and Dad some matzo ball soup and homemade Jewish crackers to the store to help them celebrate the Jewish New Year. Mom and Dad, in return, would give them some bananas. The Hong family members always looked forward every year for the Jewish New Year.
>
> One of my brothers shared Kibee, a Lebanese food with the Mike Kattawar family, who was our next door neighbor. Louise Dorsey, a Black lady, who lived across the street from the store, would cook some neck bones with turnip greens and cornbread. She would bring some to the store for us to eat. [166]

While situations like these may have been rare, that they can exist gives testimony to the power of positive interpersonal contact in transcending the negative stereotypes of racial prejudice and discrimination and offers hope for a more equalitarian society.

---

[166] Shirley Hong Woo Kwan. "Growing Up in the Mississippi Delta."

8. Growing Up Chinese in the Delta

Not surprisingly, most children born to Delta Chinese grocers had more education, as well as higher expectations and aspirations, than their immigrant parents. They were not content to accept their lives as second-class citizens in the small towns in Arkansas and Mississippi of the Delta. However, there was some variation in how American-born Chinese felt about their Delta roots, what their social status was, how they sought to improve their futures in the Delta, and whether they elected to move to a different region of the country.

More than a few, especially those from the second and later generations left the region, many with a mixture of regret and relief. Some left to escape the lack of opportunity and limited social status while others left for better educational, employment and professional opportunities. They found better acceptance and new opportunities elsewhere, which did not exist or were unavailable in the Delta, at least to Chinese. Yet, for all their misgivings, most of those who moved away still retained an unusually steadfast fondness and emotional bond to many of their past connections to the Delta.

Among those who spent most, if not all, of their years living in the Delta, some were unable to leave because of personal and business reasons and learned to make the best of their situation. Over the years, their lives improved as positive social changes occurred. There were also others who remained because they were very satisfied with their lives in the Delta and saw no need to leave. They felt they could have successful careers and businesses without having to leave.

Sam Sue of Clarksdale

Sam Sue, born and raised in Clarksdale, left eventually to pursue a Ph.D. in educational psychology at the City University of New York. In 1991, Sam wrote about the alienation he felt while he was growing up in Mississippi. Early in life he recognized the racial barriers and struggled to discover and deal with where Chinese stood in the racial fabric. [167]

> As a kid, I remember going to the theatre and not really knowing where I was supposed to sit. Blacks were segregated then. Colored people had to sit upstairs, and white people sat downstairs. I didn't know where I was supposed to sit, so I sat in the white section, and nobody said anything. So I always had to confront those problems growing up. So these experiences were very painful.
>
> I guess I was always considered marginal with whites and blacks, though I think I got along better with blacks. I really didn't have any childhood friends. I just felt I had nothing in common with them. And I guess I felt there was this invisible barrier.

He learned soon that Chinese stood somewhere between the whites at the top and the blacks at the bottom of the social ladder:

> Blacks were at the very low end of the scale, and the Chinese were sort of in between. We didn't really fit in. Very rich, aristocratic whites were at the top end. Chinese really didn't have a place in society. Economically they were better than the blacks, but on a social scale, they didn't amount to very much. I think blacks saw us as Jews. We were in the same position as Jews were in the town. We all sort of played marginal economic roles. There were quite a few Jews in town. They weren't accepted by blacks or whites either. I don't think whites knew what to make of us.

---

[167] Sam Sue. "Growing up in Mississippi." In *Asian American Experiences in the United States: Oral histories.* ed. J. Faung and J. Lee (Jefferson, N. C.: Farland), 3-9.

Sam did not even feel comfortable with Chinese exclusivity of social contact, a fact that only reinforced the view that Chinese had a lower status in society.

> Chinese church was more of a social, rather than a religious event. I always hated the gatherings. I was basically ashamed of being Chinese. I think that's probably true for a lot of Chinese Americans _ on the east and west coast. Whether they will acknowledge it is something else. But I think there is a lot of self-hatred, induced by society, culture, and circumstances. So I hated to go to these Chinese parties. Besides, it's not like you could date any Chinese girls, because they were all your cousins.

Growing up, Sam felt that even being identified as a Southerner was painful.

> I remember customers telling my dad, "Your son sounds like a Yankee." I think I had a Southern drawl, but it wasn't pronounced. I also mimicked northern accents because I was so alienated.

His experiences in Mississippi did not allow him to acquire a strong knowledge of Chinese culture, its customs and values.

> I didn't learn how to use chopsticks until I left Mississippi. We never used chopsticks at home. I didn't even have any idea of what a Chinese restaurant was until I went to college. My first encounter with a Chinese restaurant was in Cleveland, Ohio. There just weren't any near where I was growing up.

> I can't speak the language, and you feel intimidated by it when you go into restaurants. Like you keep ordering the same dishes because those are the only dishes you can order. You feel that since you are Chinese, you should be able to speak to other people that look like you. Sometimes they have mistaken me for a *juk-kok* (foreign-born Chinese) and started talking to me; I can't understand a word.

I don't feel Chinese, and I'm not. I identify myself as Asian American. I feel Chinese to some extent, but not necessarily to the extent of knowing much about Chinese culture or tradition. When I was in college, I met these Asian studies majors, and there was a certain amount of resentment, in that they could speak the language and know the culture, but they didn't know what it was like to be Chinese in a white society. They may have had a superficial understanding of the culture and language, but at that time I sort of felt they were expropriating our culture, and I felt very possessive about other Asian women. It's like when I walk outside, I know I will be treated differently. It's not something I like saying. It's not even a political statement. It's just seeing reality. I'm not looking for, or am I supersensitive to, being treated as a Chinese person, or a non-white person, but it's there. It's even here in New York.

In 1991, Sam concluded with this pessimistic outlook about a future for him as a Chinese in the Delta:

> "I left Mississippi in 1973. There was no future for me there. I was so alienated that even if I thought there was something concrete to be done there, I have such bad feelings for the place I wouldn't go back. Being Chinese in Mississippi was definitely a handicap."

Bobby Joe Moon of Boyle

Born in 1942 in Boyle, Bobby Joe Moon grew up in the family operated grocery. After college, he moved to Houston, Texas, where he now lives and works as an accountant. The following excerpts are some of his reflections in an open letter he addressed to his niece several years ago and posted on a website, *USA DEEP SOUTH* to explain what it meant to be Chinese in the segregationist Mississippi society during the time from just prior to and during the Civil Rights movement.[168]

Figure 42 Bobby Joe Moon, just one of the gang with white kids, at a classmate's birthday party. Courtesy of Bobby Joe Moon.

> There was no question that we were not White since while we were growing up in the store we saw Whites and Blacks and they were not like our family. What was puzzling was why we were allowed to go to public school in Boyle [Mississippi] with Whites and segregated from Blacks, but in Cleveland there was a Chinese School . . . pretty crazy!
>
> Even funnier was that when the Chinese kids reached high school age they were allowed to attend Cleveland High School. I remember attending Chinese-led mission church services at First Baptist Church across from the courthouse until we built our own church building on Highway 8. The White lady Sunday school teachers would come so faithfully each Sunday afternoon: Mrs. H. H. Elmore and Dr. Georgia Tatum and perhaps Mrs. Elizabeth Murray in later years.

---

[168] Bobby Joe Moon. Growing up in Mississippi in the '40s – '60s. *http://usads.ms11.net/bjm.html*

Think of the situation: We lived in the Black neighborhood for business purposes but went to school with Whites. We had to become adept at balancing between Blacks and Whites. We Chinese were allowed into both worlds, but we mainly stayed among ourselves. We were in both worlds but not of both worlds. We knew we were not to date girls of either world. We made our livelihoods from the Blacks primarily and from some Whites.

In public school we (my brothers and I) competed well with Whites: Jimmy was valedictorian of his class, William and I were honor students as well as American Legion Boys' State representatives. I was the recipient of several other awards such as the Kossman Award and the Danforth Award. When Jimmy came through the eleventh grade a few years later, they changed the rules for Boys' State participants and only allowed boys whose fathers were American Legion members . . .hmm, what's up here?

In Greenville the Chinese kids were mistreated as well -- even when they earned the highest grade averages in public school they were not allowed to be named valedictorians!

And how about such mundane things as haircuts? I did not even get a professional haircut until I was 15 years old because I always got my haircuts from Dad or Kam Joe. Why was it that way? In the early days when Chinese came to Mississippi, the White barbers refused to cut the Chinese's hair and sent them to the Black barbershops. The Chinese chose to cut their own hair.

How about the days of having separate waiting rooms and drinking fountains for Blacks and Whites? Confusing again for us -- but we were bold enough to use the White facilities including the White section in movie theaters. What a crazy world of race and prejudices in the '40s, '50s, and '60s!

Racial climate: We could sense the growing tension between Blacks and Whites as we were growing up in the late '50s and early '60s leading up to the Civil Rights Freedom Marches. Being in the White world for public schools, our parents had to donate money to the White Citizens' Council and yet try to be supportive of the Blacks from whom they were making their livelihoods. Again, this was very confusing for us. We were taught to hate the Blacks by being in the White world. We were taught that Dr. Martin Luther King Jr. was a Communist. I thought the South was going to have a Civil War between the Blacks and Whites when Emmett Till was lynched.

The biggest event of our generation happened when I was still at Mississippi State University -- the assassination of President John F. Kennedy. The response was again crazy: When news of the shooting was announced there was whooping and hollering in jubilation by the White boys in our dormitory! I said to myself, "These people are nuts! Let me out of here!" I knew I could never live in my home state anymore and couldn't wait to graduate since it was my ticket to get out of there.

In fact, I did graduate one year early in three years with my degree in accounting. Don't get me wrong, I cherish my life growing up and getting my education in the Magnolia State, but these are but some of the events that shaped me and affected me even as an adult today. I'll always be proud to be from Mississippi, but we were intelligent enough to leave.

Nancy Bing Chew of Lula

In Lula, a small town of several hundred people, Nancy Bing Chew's parents owned the Joe Bing Grocery, one of the four Chinese grocery stores there. Growing up in a small town in the 1940s was not the most exciting or stimulating place for her. Most people in her town seemed content or satisfied with their existence, with no apparent ambition for achieving higher goals.

The racial prejudices of the region had not yet been challenged, and Chinese children were not treated well by some teachers who discriminated against them for their eagerness to success in school, but overall, she and other Chinese got along with classmates. Still, Chinese relationships with townspeople were strictly based on their daily business interactions in the grocery store, and there were not many social friendships among Chinese with whites.

Nancy recalled wanting wider opportunities in life than she dreamed possible in a conservative community that held many narrow-minded beliefs and attitudes.

> I always was a rebellious and outspoken person. My views sometimes clashed with popular conventions. I was not a 'religious' person in the usual sense, but I attended church regularly when I was growing up because of social norms. I felt that many of the most devout people were hypocrites. My parents did not believe in Christian beliefs but they let us go to church because some of the white customers urged them.

> After I finished high school in 1960, I left the Delta for college. I only applied to California schools, and decided to attend the University of Southern California. Coming from a high school with a graduating class of only 10 students, and immediately attending university classes with several hundred students, was a bit overwhelming at first. Even though I was not the best student in the world, I enjoyed the stimulation of the many new ideas I was learning.

Nancy managed to adapt successfully, however, and delighted in the wider diversity, tolerance, and openness in California. Still, after college and marriage, Nancy returned to Clarksdale with her husband from California and helped her parents operate their grocery store.

However, the contrast between the Delta and California lifestyles became much more apparent than she had realized previously, and after three years, she and her husband returned to California. She found living in the Delta was too restricting and lacking in diversity and stimulation.[169]

Bonnie Lew of Clarksdale

Now retired from a career as a librarian in Stockton, California, Bonnie Lew was born and raised in San Francisco. In 1964 when she was 8 years old, her family moved to Mississippi to work with relatives in a grocery store in Boyle, and then in Clarksdale. The transition involved a difficult adjustment, and she did not enjoy her experiences there as an adolescent. For example, when she and her brother first arrived in Mississippi, they did not do well in school, especially in math, and had to attend summer school.

Bonnie reflected on her unsettling encounters with racial discrimination there in an interview conducted in 1982,[170]

> Apparently it was only two years prior to our move that the Chinese could go to school with the whites. So I attended a school that was strictly white with a few Chinese. I was treated fine when I was in grammar school. In fact, when I was in the sixth grade, I was invited to a couple of birthday parties. These parties were given by a lot of the rich, white Southern families in town whose children were in school with me. But as soon as I got into junior high school, all social activities stopped and I was ignored, period. Maybe it was because I was Chinese, or maybe I was unattractive, or maybe I didn't have the brightest personality in the world.

[169]Nancy Bing Chew, Interview by John Jung, June 26, 2008.
[170] Bonnie C. Lew. "I always felt out of place there. Growing up Chinese in Mississippi." In *Chinese American Voices: From the gold rush to the present,* ed. Judy Yung, Gordon H. Chang & Him Mark Lai. (Berkeley and Los Angeles, Ca.: University of California Press, 2006), 281-291.

It didn't hit me that it was really discrimination until I went back to the same high school to teach after college. The mothers of the students that I had been shunned by the whole time that I was in the seventh through the twelfth grade, were coming up to me and saying, "Oh, you're Miss Cheung, weren't you in Troy's class?" and calling me "Ma'am" and this whole bit. And they had been the same ones that had not even looked my way. It was really difficult to handle because I knew inside what they really felt. But because my status had changed and because I was now a teacher of their children, they were treating me with respect (pp. 284-285).

Bonnie witnessed the racial inequality and injustices in Mississippi and had to figure out for herself where Chinese stood between whites and blacks.

If you lived in the South and saw the blacks the time we were growing up...of course, a lot of it is different now, a lot of them are more educated...many of them were illiterate. You know, my mother signed more welfare checks, it was her handwriting on the back of one million and ten of them. And once, one of the women had her daughter sign the back of the check, and the check came back to her and they said, "Hey, this is not the same person. Did you get your money?" She said, "Oh, no, no. Miss Tom used to sign my checks for me, but I got my daughter to sign it because she can write now." They would come in just to cash their checks and buy two dollars' worth of groceries, and we would charge them a dime to sign and cash their check. That was a lot of dimes. My mom use to say, "Geez, they must think my name is Hattie Lou Smith."(laughs) But it was strictly business-that was all. Although I had one black friend that I used to run around with, and her name was Baby Lou. My parents didn't mind because I would run over to Louise's house and run back. I didn't stay gone very long, maybe an hour or so It was very seldom that we would play with the black kids. A lot of them were very dirty. Even as a child I knew that I didn't want to associate with a lot of them. They lived in poverty and it was not something that they could really help, you know, when you have just one faucet in the house. I was growing up in a black neighborhood that was really poor. We had ditches and gravel on the street, the whole bit, it was like living out in the country. It wasn't until 1963 that they paved the street in front of our house, and it was a city street. It's hard to tell you how it's like. The mud just rushing in with the water after the rain and stuff like that.

You know, everyone has to have someone to be better than … I mean no matter whether you're a poor black living in a rat-infested hole, you're better than somebody out there. The blacks were the only people that the Chinese could be better than. The whites were on top, and we were squished in the middle. I came home from school one time all fired up about something political. It must have been from American government or civics class; I don't even remember what it was. I just remember the comment my father made, "You don't talk about them (the whites) like that. You're Chinese and you have nowhere to go." He knew his place, and essentially he was right. You can't go down, you definitely couldn't go up at that time. I can't remember whether I was in the ninth grade or twelfth grade at the time, but I remember the comment more than anything else. Later when I returned to California, I noticed that prejudice was more blatant here. They do it to your face, whereas in Mississippi you knew your place or you knew where everybody belonged. A funny thing, my father used to fish so much in the summer that he would get very dark. He was refused service at a couple of restaurants when he walked in with his white friends because they thought he was black. Chinese were not stopped from going anywhere the whites were as long as you looked lighter. That's just how it was and you just lived with it. It was just all part of growing up (pp. 288-289).

Sung Gay Chow of Boyle

Now living in Pennsylvania, Sung Gay Chow is a professor who teaches Asian American and Southern studies courses at Indiana University. Back in 1986, when he lived in the Delta, he lamented that Chinese youth did not feel they were accepted in the Delta.[171]

> But for us adolescents, we were sensitive to the fact that we were different and that we were considered second-class citizens, more or less. The social status of the Chinese, I think, has always been low (although not as low as that of the blacks).
>
> My generation learned early how fixed the racial and social boundaries were. We soon understood that there were rules-most of them unwritten-that required everyone to toe the line.

Although well treated and accepted by whites when they were children, once they reached adolescence, social relationships abruptly shifted along race lines, and Chinese received second-class status.

> As children, some of us had been able to crawl underneath both fences and see what each society was like. We could even play with, the other kids. But as we grew older_ it was the seventh grade for me _ these kids, now teenagers, began to ignore us. Now, we had to be content just to look through the cracks of the fence and see what white society was doing that we couldn't participate in any longer. Ironically, we treated blacks the same way. We thus made our way down a narrow path between two fences, one that kept the blacks apart from us and another, which kept us from the whites.

---

[171] Sung Gay Chow. "A Personal View of the Mississippi Chinese." In *Mississippi Writers: Reflections of Childhood and Youth*, Vol. II, ed. D. Abbot. (Jackson, MS: University Press of Mississippi, 1985), 75-97.

These ethnic/racial barriers were reciprocal in that Chinese parents did not expect that they would ever receive equal treatment in white society.

> One should understand, too, that many Chinese prefer life that way. All three races are different, they say, and it's futile trying to integrate them. Sure, you might be able to do it to a certain extent but never, ever, fully. Not yet anyway. You can do business with each other. You might be able to exchange pleasantries with each other on the street. But you won't have the kind of relationship that is indicative of people who truly interact. The majority of people of Mississippi, I think, accept this coexistence without question.

Inevitably, as the Chinese youth tried to negotiate entry into mainstream society they came into conflict at times with the goals their parents held for them. Neither generation understood or embraced the other generation's ways of thinking.

> To the despair of our parents, we aspired to be assimilated into white society. What we learned and what we became during and after college distanced us from our parents and our heritage. We formed certain perspectives, held different interests, and had conflicting attitudes, which set us apart from the previous generation. After college, some of us did return to the Delta and worked in the family store. Others also stayed in Mississippi but worked in occupations unrelated to the grocery business.

One solution for Chinese youth was to become professionals using their higher education to achieve more material success and seek community acceptance. However, Chow felt that there would always be a racial barrier or gap beyond which Chinese could not pass in a white dominated society.

Those who continue to live in Mississippi have tried hard to become part of the white community. Being upwardly mobile, some have left the small stores in the black neighborhoods and have opened larger ones on the other side of town. Others, having left the grocery business to their fathers, have become pharmacists, computer programmers, and engineers. Still others have their own businesses, such as gift shops, restaurants, and television repair shops. They have joined civic organizations and have become members of churches. They do charity work, host parties, and give dinners. Some even have an interest in local politics. An increasing number have married members of the white community.

I question, though, whether my generation has really "made it." It is a delusion to think that just because we have gotten out of the store and into pharmacy or engineering we have been accepted into white society. True, the fact that we are economically successful does count for something, but money is only one measure of power and only a minimal means of entrance into white Mississippi society. I think the members of my generation understand that, although they may not admit it.

Sung Gay speculated that a deep-seated fear of social rejection led Chinese to enter professions and occupations that did not involve confrontation with the power structure of society.

Take, for example, the occupations some Chinese choose. While they may be employed in high-paying jobs, it is doubtful if any will rise to high management positions that require decision- or policy-making, which is an expression of power in any level of society. Moreover it seems to me that Chinese know or anticipate risks (such as discrimination) involved in desiring to move upwards in white society.

They thus choose disciplines such as engineering and accounting, where they can keep a low profile. The fear of discrimination, too, perhaps accounts for the rarity of

Mississippi Chinese in law and medicine, which are socially prestigious professions within the community. In addition, some Chinese may see themselves as too passive or acquiescent to deal directly with patients and clients.

Like the rest of Mississippi, the Chinese are pretty conservative in their lifestyle and politics. Because they are slow to accept change, they prefer to maintain the status quo. Instead of being vocal or assertive, they remain passive and pragmatic. Instead of forcing the issue, they wait for the opportunity for change to present itself. They would rather work within the system than outside it.

Sung Gay saw some irony in that Delta Chinese are conservative and accede to social traditions. He concluded that Chinese outdo many white southerners themselves in being southern in their outlook on life.

Of course, one can say people in other sections of the country also emphasize family, tradition, and a conservative way of life. True, but these traits are more closely identified with the South. One can also say that such traits are characteristically Chinese. However, these attributes are even more strongly reinforced in the Chinese who live in Mississippi. None of the young Mississippi Chinese act like their counterparts elsewhere. For example, the Chinese in California, especially in San Francisco, act more assertively and are more aggressive in their ethnicity. And in the Chinatowns of other cities like San Francisco, street gangs thrive.

With the South as a region changing so rapidly, it is interesting to note that Mississippi Chinese in some ways show more resistance to change, and in this respect they are perhaps more traditionally southern than many southerners. I suggest that environment has a lot to do with those similarities between the Chinese and the prevalent culture.

He concluded with the observation that despite the distasteful history of being relegated to lower social status, the Delta Chinese still hold a fondness for their Delta roots.

> It is a sense of place __ and that place being Mississippi__, which reinforces our cultural values and ideals. And while the Mississippi Chinese seem to be disowned or dislocated, we are certainly not detached. We have roots embedded in this place as well.

Sherman Hong of Greenville

Born and raised in Greenville where his family had a grocery store, Sherman Hong grew up during a transition period full of strife and tension when Jim Crow began to be challenged by civil rights activism of the 1960s. Nonetheless, he was able to assimilate with relative ease and achieve a successful professional career in music and blend readily into mainstream white society. Until his retirement in 2005, he was a faculty member at the University of Southern Mississippi in Hattiesburg for 40 years where he and his Caucasian wife, Mildred, raised their family. He feels well-accepted there and enjoys living in his community, where he serves as the conductor of the City of Hattiesburg Concert Band. Although as a child, he had a few negative encounters with prejudice against Chinese, by and large, he feels these problems were minimal and that attitudes regarding Chinese are highly favorable in his community.

Much of this success, in Sherman's view, began with his positive childhood experiences growing up in a multi-racial neighborhood:

> My assimilation into the Caucasian society was shaped by the attitudes and relationships developed due to the location of my parent's grocery store. Unlike most Chinese grocery stores situated in black neighborhoods, our store was in a

unique location. On our side of the block neighbors were Syrian, Lebanese, and Caucasians (including a Jewish family). On the side of the store and across the street were Caucasian homes, but directly behind them were rows of black homes. Directly across the street were a couple of homes for whites, but next to them were two rows of shotgun houses occupied by black families. The entire neighborhood can be classified as fairly poor and blue collar. Our customers consisted of neighbors of many races.

Another important factor was the opportunity to learn about the world outside of the Delta by meeting and talking with many people from other regions of the country, often with different attitudes and values from those he encountered previously.

> Greenville at that time (1940s) had an air force base that brought in servicemen and their families from around the country. Additionally, the Port of Greenville was nearby, and some of the Mississippi River towboats docked there. The result was that in addition to our neighbors, we encountered customers from the air force base and towboat crewmen.

> Another happenstance was that the couple who supervised the trailer park was an inter-racial couple—he was a Caucasian married to a Choctaw Indian woman. All those influences combined to develop my tolerance and open-mindedness. In essence, we had a "multi-ethnic" neighborhood.

These experiences taught him that harmonious relationships can exist among people of different races, even in the segregated South. He recalled that as a child, he freely played with both whites and blacks.

> ...As young boys we would play pickup games of both baseball and football...It frequently happened that our pickup team of neighborhood whites and Chinese boys would play games against a pickup team of black neighbors

...We had no fighting and had only the normal sports banter between the races.

I attended the neighborhood "white" elementary school about two blocks from our store...There was minimal derisive talk directed toward me; in fact I was just another elementary student to about 99% of the kids. I must give credit to the teachers and the open-mindedness of children for this transitional period. I went on to success there and even was elected student council president.

Sherman felt he was blessed to have musical talent. He acknowledged that his talent in music was the single most important factor that opened doors for him and acceptance in the "white" society.

I think the greatest move in acceptance occurred when in junior high school. Here we were out of our neighborhood school and socialized with kids from all over the town. Thus did my associations begin with youth from the "better and best parts" of town.

The success I had in band led to many band trips and being selected to attend honor bands in different parts of the state—this eliminated the provincialism of staying in a restricted geographical area...My continuing success led to being in the select Lion's All State Band three consecutive years. The band was all Caucasian, except for me. In Greenville I was asked by a prominent merchant and musician to be a part of his efforts at starting the Greenville Symphony. Through those years I came into contact with musicians from throughout the region and began to learn orchestral literature...

Along with four of my Caucasian friends, we formed a rock band after seeing a traveling show that came to perform at our high school. Little did we know that those visiting groups would go on to fame. Their music was "strange" to us, but we quickly loved it. That show consisted of Roy Orbison, Carl Perkins, Jerry Lee Lewis (yes-he did knock over the piano bench when he played!), and Johnny Cash and their respective bands.

Yet during the era when he was growing up, Sherman was a victim at times of the racial prejudices and segregation that were still prevalent in the region. He described two vivid incidents.

> While still in elementary school, I suddenly became ill in the classroom. My folks rushed me to our doctor who diagnosed that my appendix was about to burst. I was rushed to the black hospital, where my Caucasian doctor successfully performed surgery... But because I was young, this prejudicial action made little impression on me.
>
> ...The following incident brought that reality to me quite forcefully. Once while we were playing (sandlot football), Chuck, my youngest brother, got hit in the face and his glasses were broken. Pieces of glass went in one eye. We rushed him to the nearest hospital emergency room. Because he wasn't Caucasian, they refused him emergency services and we had to seek help elsewhere. I believe that this was the first time I was made strongly aware of segregation and prejudice.

Despite advances in social standing for racial minorities during the 1960s, interracial dating remained a taboo in most places in the country. Interracial marriage was even rarer, especially in the Delta.

> I don't recall interracial dating. We observed and had good social contacts but no thoughts of dating across racial lines because of the furor it would create.

> After high school I attended what is now the University of Southern Mississippi...I had many Caucasian lady friends and eventually began dating some of them. Race differences never reared its head except once. The girl I was seriously dating broke-up with me because her father promised to give her a car (by the way, the father was in North Carolina and *not* Mississippi).

While teaching as an instructor there in 1965, and working on a doctorate, he began dating and soon fell in love with Mildred Sterling, a undergraduate singer who would go on to win the 1966 Metropolitan Opera Regional Auditions.

> As a young couple of different races, we knew that our respective fathers would be difficult. Of course at this time there were few, if any, thoughts of lawfully sanctioned inter-racial marriages in the state. My father wanted me to marry a Chinese girl and her father wanted a Caucasian son-in-law. My father characterized white girls as lazy and money hungry, so he really tried to discourage me.

Love prevailed, and the marriage not only took place, but they were very successful in winning over the parents-in-law of both the bride and groom. Being an interracial couple did not appear to present major problems, and in some respects, Sherman acknowledged it had some advantages.

> With Mildred's singing and acting talents, she became well-known to the "right" people in Hattiesburg Society. Because of her, I can also say I know and socialize with many of them and no one seems to think of race—to them I'm just Sherman. In fact, some of our friends told me they never knew I was Chinese.

Sherman believes that growing up Chinese in the Mississippi Delta in the evolving 1940s and 1950s "afforded me a wide variety of life influencing experiences, for I was an active participant in Chinese, Caucasian, and even black societies."[172]

Conclusion

---

[172] Sherman Hong. "Growing Up in the Mississippi Delta," Unpublished, 2008.

These compelling narratives describe a spectrum of ways that American-born Chinese dealt with and reacted to the experiences of growing up being of Chinese descent in the Delta. From an outsider's view, it seems clear that all of them, to varying extents, encountered incidents of racial prejudice against Chinese as they grew up in the 1940s and 1950s. Yet, there were wide variations in how they reacted to these threats and the extent to which these experiences harmed their psychological well-being and self-esteem.

All of these individuals who shared their stories, fortunately, were strong enough to endure the pain and not succumb as victims. Some realized that life was not always fair, but rather than dwell in despair on what they had little or no control over, they responded by focusing on education, an area that they could control. They were able to move on to be successful despite these obstacles, but it is likely that many lacked the ability to overcome these threats.

The presence of strong family support among Chinese in the Delta also helped buffer these threats so that their children could emerge with self-esteem despite the oppressive discrimination. In fact, some did not even regard themselves as victimized by racism even if outsiders held such views.[173] Some stayed in the Delta for most if not all of their lives but many others searched for and resettled in places that recognized, respected, and valued diversity.

---

[173] See Leslie Bow (2007). "Meditations of the partly colored." *Southern Review*, 43,1: 89-95. This essay by a daughter of Chinese grocer parents from the Delta, who grew up on the West Coast, illustrates the irreconcilable differences between her perceptions and those of her parents about the social reality of Delta prejudice toward Chinese. Perhaps, to paraphrase Rudyard Kipling, "South is South, and West is West…"

9. Chinese Identity And Community

Once their children were admitted to white public schools, where many, if not most, were excellent students, the Chinese received more respect and began to be better treated by white society. Chinese were permitted to buy and live in homes in white neighborhoods where they had been previously excluded. When the children finished high school, many entered and graduated from universities. Many embarked into professional careers and others opened businesses. These gains in their social status led some observers to conclude that the Delta Chinese wanted to acquire white values and become assimilated to mainstream American society, as suggested in the left side of Figure 43.

In areas where discrimination against Chinese American excluded their participation, they seem to have developed parallel institutions modeled after the white, rather than black, style and format.[174] Church services, for example, adopted the rituals and practices of white churches. Chinese cemeteries, like white cemeteries, had a section for deceased infants and children. The Chinese school used the curriculum and teaching methods found in white schools. On the social level, Chinese youth embraced white rather than black styles of dancing at their parties, where white bands perform.

While the Chinese merchants did learn enough English to be able to conduct business and adopted many customs and traditions of whites, they still maintained strong ties to their Chinese culture, as shown in the right side of the diagram below. The immigrant generations did not aspire

---

[174] James W. Loewen, *The Mississippi Chinese*.

to become Americanized if it meant relinquishing their Chinese customs and traditions. And, although they fought a losing battle, they tried to instill Chinese values among their American-born children who were torn between two cultures.

These words of one grocer clearly expresses the outlook held by many of the Chinese who came to the Delta prior to the 1950s:

> We stick together, work, and don't bother nobody. We don't mix with nobody, we keep our mouth shut, no talk, just work…We didn't want to become *Bok Guey* [whites] and we sure don't want to become "colored" like the *Hok Guey* [blacks], no sir, those people were treated worse than dogs. We don't want that to happen to us anyhow, anywhere, anyway. We just want to be ourselves, *Hon Yen* [Chinese].[175]

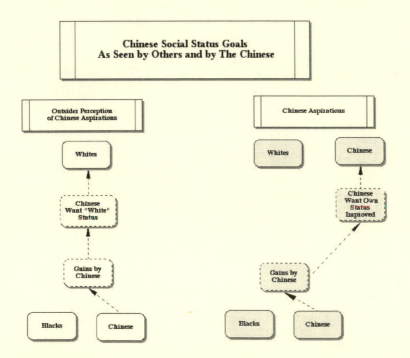

Figure 43 Outsider View (left) of Chinese Immigrant Goals vs. Chinese View (right)

---

[175] Robert Seto Quan, *Lotus Among the Magnolias*, 43-44.

Although few of the original immigrants were able to return to Guangdong after Communist China came to power in 1949, as noted in an earlier chapter, they had come to the United States with the intention of returning after they had earned their fortunes on Gold Mountain. With limited prospects of ever returning to China, they resigned themselves to make the best of the situation by trying to preserve their cultural practices and values despite their ethnic isolation and to foster a Chinese identity in their children.

The early Chinese immigrants in the Delta did not seek to assimilate into either black or white society as they wanted to retain their Chinese identity and eventually return to China. Chinese wanted to avoid being equated with blacks that held the lowest status in a highly segregated society. They did not want to be white, but wanted the equality of status with whites. They tried to instill and create a Chinese identity in their American-born children, who were becoming increasingly assimilated to white values and customs.

The observations of Sam Sue who grew up in the back of his parents' grocery store in Clarksdale illustrate the difficulty of drawing conclusions about all Chinese grocers. His parents did *not* support the view that Chinese aspired to 'white' status, but he allowed that other Chinese may have had such a goal.[176]

> I think it is an overgeneralization and to some extent a misrepresentation to say that immigrant Chinese wanted to be white. I think they just wanted to be well off financially but essentially still Chinese. I saw no effort on my father's part to become a part of the white society. They wanted their children to be Chinese.

---

[176] Sam Sue, e-mail message to Author, Jan. 20, 2008.

However, the better off Chinese families who ran "supermarkets"—such as the Wongs were more assimilated---they were located in white areas, could speak English fairly well. They may have wanted to become more assimilated within the dominant white power structure.

The view that Chinese grocers had their own hierarchy based on their financial success and degree of assimilation to white values was confirmed by interviews with 25 Chinese grocers and 50 non Chinese in several Delta communities.[177]

> The wealthier Chinese in these larger towns have adjusted to a total society relationship with the town, whereas the poorer Chinese with their smaller stores and limited incomes have maintained their ethnic identification, and have had it reinforced by their constant social and economic associations with the Negro community…These variations of interests and goal directions have led to a type of class split among the Chinese in these larger towns. Chinese themselves admitted that a type of class structure exists (among themselves) but they felt it was for the good of both parties concerned.

The contention was that the wealthier merchants had more modern stores that followed the white supermarket model as they aspired to white acceptance. In contrast, it was felt that smaller and less profitable grocers in the black neighborhoods retained a stronger Chinese identity. These grocers also failed to distance themselves from blacks, and hence weakened acceptance of all Chinese by the white power structure.

Immigrants Maintained Chinese Identity

The immigrants went to considerable lengths to stay connected with relatives and family in their villages in China. They did not forsake

---

[177] Rummel, "Delta Chinese," 36-37.

their parents and relatives in China, but made regular remittances to help support their families. They made return visits to marry. Afterwards they returned to visit wives and children if they had not already brought them to the U. S. Later, some sent their American-born children to China for their education prior to the start of World War II, especially when it was denied to them in the U.S.

Many Chinese immigrants in the Delta, as in other parts of the country, subscribed to Chinese newspapers from San Francisco, Chicago, or New York to help them stay informed about what was going on in the world related to China.

They preferred to cook their meals in the Chinese stir-fry style rather than using American methods. They purchased Chinese food ingredients such as fermented bean cakes, herbal medicine such as Tiger Balm and po chai, rice wine *ng ga py*, and many grew their own Chinese vegetables such as winter melon or bitter melon in their back yards. They ordered Chinese household goods such as dishes and decorations that were unavailable in the Delta from Chinatown merchants in San Francisco or Chicago.

> We raised chickens to provide fresh eggs, as well as for dinner. My parents made salt fish with procedures used in China for drying and preserving fish, which they hung in the sun in their back yard. They ate many traditional Chinese foods like seaweed soup, sai fuun, fu jook, and preserved lichee nuts obtained by mail order from San Francisco. They also grew their own Chinese vegetables such as foo qua (bitter melon) and dit qua, oong gua (winter melon), which were unavailable in local stores.[178]

---

[178] Leland Gion, Interview with John Jung, Oct. 26, 2007.

Folk medicine remedies and concepts such as the health benefits of maintaining a balance of yin and yang forces by eating both "hot" and "cold" foods were retained even as many aspects of Western medicine were adopted.

Chinese immigrants may have learned enough about American culture to survive, but they preferred to practice and retain their Chinese traditions and customs in their family and community life.

One striking example of the community bonds that existed among the Chinese grocers was that a social gathering was held whenever one of them decided to build a house for their family.

> There would be parties when each Chinese family was finally able to build a decent house to live in (rather than live in the back of the store). Someone would set up a gas burner in the garage and cook and families from throughout the Delta area would come, e.g., a party in Marks would bring Chinese from Clarksdale, and as far as Memphis and Greenwood (2-3 hours away).[179]

In the view of Sam Sue:

> The immigrant Chinese preserved their identity through kinship. In my father's hometown and neighboring areas, many, not all, of the Chinese came from the same village and were related. We had cousins in Clarksdale (the Joe's), another in Marks and one in Jonestown (the Chin's) and in Greenwood and Memphis. Our parents would pay weekly or biweekly visits to their stores to chat and catch up.
>
> Our parents did very little to assimilate and there was little basis for assimilating even if one assumed the motive. Our parents simply couldn't speak English well enough to be understood. My mother and father had no resources with which to learn the English language. My father did most of

---

[179] Sam Sue, e-mail message to Author, Jan. 21, 2008.

his business in a rural southern black English. He needed English on a functional level, which never went above a grade school reading level. My mother's English skills were even poorer—she spoke relatively little and she could probably hardly read English though she was literate in Chinese (in fact she had received a fairly high level of education for a woman in China before she left China to live with my father).

What they understood about the world was through the Chinese language newspapers such as the Chinese Times mailed to them from San Francisco.[180]

Fostering A Chinese Identity in Children

Chinese immigrants instilled Chinese customs and values in their children. Parents taught respect for Confucian values, respect for elders, parental authority, and a patriarchal family structure.

Sam Sue observed that:

Many of the values of hard work, piety toward elders were instilled in us all. Our "Chineseness" was instilled by the fact that we "felt" apart from others and from what we experienced as children of Chinese immigrants. Unlike others, we had to deal with the fact that our parents with limited English proficiency didn't bother to teach us the Chinese language. This wasn't particularly common among the other Chinese families (or at least that's how I felt) and there was this big unfilled space in communication between our parents and their children (our oldest brother could speak Chinese).[181]

As Frances Wong from Louise explained, her mother emphasized Confucian concepts of conduct in her children:

My mother was always teaching us. She always used the Confucius scene, the proud words of the old Chinese. She used proud words and Confucianism to teach us. She would

---

[180] Ibid.
[181] Ibid.

always taught (sic) us to be honest and to be generous, She taught us never to be greedy...Always be polite and always honor your elders. Always try to be helpful, and always be good. That is part of the training we received. From what she taught me in the old sayings in Chinese, I still use it today.[182]

The language spoken at home typically was Chinese because many parents generally did not speak much English. Parents wanted children to learn to at least be able to converse in Chinese. Even if their children did not speak it, they could comprehend what their parents were saying in Chinese. Some parents made efforts to have their children attend Chinese schools here, or in China, so they could acquire the Chinese language and culture.

Other parents felt that the priority for their children was to learn English and did not emphasize the learning of the Chinese language. Some may have felt that attending both American and Chinese schools in addition to helping in the store was too demanding for their children.

Shirley Hong Woo Kwan's description of how she attended both American and Chinese schools shows how demanding it was:

> Immediately after attending the school from 9 a.m.-3:30 p.m. with the White teacher, some of us would stay at the school from 4-7 p.m. learning Chinese lessons taught by Dr. Irving Woo. Later on his wife took over the class. We would meet everyday after school and on Saturday from 8-12 noon. Usually on Saturday there would be a vocabulary test. The cost for the Chinese school was only $8.00 a month.
>
> Each student was given a Chinese textbook. We had to memorize our lessons and recite them to Mrs. Woo. If we missed a word, she would tap our hand with a ruler.

---

[182] Frances Wong , Interview, Jan. 19, 2000 .

During the week Mrs. Woo gave us some vocabulary word to read and write. Every Saturday, we were given a written test on the words. She would grade them and after a few weeks she issued report cards to us. [183]

This pride in Chinese heritage often extended to third and later generations. Shirley and Richard Kwan's son, Randy expressed it as follows:

My parents always maintained that we should be proud of our Chinese heritage. They bought many books for my siblings on the history of China. We religiously watched all of the documentaries on PBS that flowed from China once President Nixon encouraged Chairman Mao Zedong to drop the veil that his China from the world.[184]

Value of Education

The Chinese placed an emphasis and priority on education. They saw education as the means by which their children could improve their futures. They were willing to sacrifice to provide full financial support for the educational expenses of their children so that they would not have to work while attending college.

Bobby Joe Moon's experience with such support from his parents was not uncommon:

We never received any pay for working in the store, but we never had to work any jobs to pay for our college educations. We ALWAYS got a new car when each of us graduated from college too. [185]

[183] Shirley Hong Woo Kwan. "Growing Up in the Mississippi Delta."

[184] Roderick Randell Kwan. Comments made at the Opening of the History of the Mississippi Delta Chinese Photo Exhibit, Capps Archives, Delta State University, Jan. 11, 2007.

[185] Bobby Joe Moon, e-mail message to Author, Nov. 3, 2007.

The strong emphasis on education, for example, while beneficial also could be divisive as it created status differences. Chinese, like other ethnic groups, were not immune from holding discriminatory attitudes among themselves, often along social class and education levels.

Robert Chow observed:

> I believe racial discrimination within the Chinese comes in many forms. I saw discrimination within the Chinese community based on their education and social status. If one business was laundry it was treated as lesser degree in social status compare to one that was a doctor, lawyer, or engineer. That's why the Chinese are so caught up on status even to this day. Back then, many (of the) younger generation made up their mind which university they plan to attend, following their parent footsteps and seeking the best social gathering at Ole Miss, Miss. St., LSU, Arkansas U., Alabama, Georgia, Texas, and Memphis State University.[186]

Social Life Limited to Other Chinese

The Delta Chinese had limited time for social gatherings but when they did have occasions such as celebrations they usually involved only other Chinese. Among parents, the little spare time that existed was often spent playing mah jong in the back of the store with friends who gathered after store hours or on Sundays, the lightest workday.

Weekend dances became the primary social outlet for Chinese youth See Figure 44). After working all week, Chinese adolescents sought social contact on weekends. Kids from would drive miles after work on Saturday night to attend weekend dance parties that would be held in larger towns. Through these dances, Chinese developed a close-knit network of Chinese youth that not only covered the Delta but extended to

---

[186] Robert Chow, e-mail message to Author, March 23, 2008.

Chinese in nearby southern states as well. These ties led to many marriages as well as life long friendships.

These dances were held at community facilities such as the Veterans of Foreign Wars (VFW) hall in Greenville or the American Legion Hall in Cleveland. Sometimes they might be held in the back of the warehouse of the Joe Gow Nue grocery in Greenville. Attendance was virtually all Chinese as there was little or no social mingling of Chinese with either whites or blacks in that era.

Figure 44 Chinese youth came from far and wide to weekend dances such as this one held at the VFW facilities in Greenville to meet other Chinese youth from across the South. Courtesy of Peter Joe

Below are two recollections of these dances that illustrate the important function they played on the social development of Chinese youth.

> Delta Chinese families networked for social gatherings --
> weddings, babies' red egg parties, birthdays, and funerals.
> The Chinese maintain close family ties, gathering for many
> occasions celebrating great moments in life – birth, marriage,
> significant birthdays, and death; recognized with much
> ceremony, all of it usually involving food. Talented Chinese

cooks from Delta towns prepared and served scrumptious meals for hundreds of guests. The gatherings were held in Greenville, Greenwood, Cleveland, and Clarksdale.

The Chinese kids organized dances in Cleveland at the Veteran of Foreign War (VFW). It was a unique phenomenon that Chinese kids came from far and near to meet at these gatherings; not only from the Mississippi Delta towns, but from Arkansas, Tennessee, Louisiana, Texas, Georgia, even Missouri and Illinois. The dances would begin late after stores were closed and last until wee hours in the morning. Parents normally would not allow their children to stay out that late, but they knew this was the only opportunity to meet other Chinese kids. It was all good clean fun, no alcohol, or drugs. No matter how late we were out, we were expected to be up for work in the morning. Informal (jam) sessions were record spinners with everybody bringing their 45rpm records.

During the 50s, a group of Chinese boys at Mississippi State University organized the *Lucky Eleven* club sponsoring the annual Christmas dances. This social event was the highlight of the year, culminating with the crowning of the Lucky Eleven Sweetheart or Queen. The girls wore formals and the guys were spiffy in nice suits. The Christmas dance would most likely be the event attended by the Chinese kids from distant places.

Later the Ole Miss Chinese boys and girls organized UMACA (University of Mississippi American Chinese Association) who also sponsored dances. When Sam Chu Lin was at Ole Miss, he organized the Christmas "Holiday Extravaganza" to top ALL parties, underwritten by Ole Miss Chinese students. Gradually as American Chinese college kids became more accepted and assimilated with other students on campus, the need for organizations like the Lucky Eleven and "UMACA" was no longer necessary.[187]

The Chinese kids__ when they would close the store, they would have a dance that would be real late at night. That is

---

[187] Frieda Quon, Interview, Jan.12, 2000.

where we met. All the Chinese kids would get together. They go from different towns. They would have a dance in Cleveland or they would have a dance in Greenville. There would be a dance at Helena, Arkansas. Kids from all over Arkansas, Mississippi, and Louisiana. Chinese children would drive, and they would attend the dance there. That is how we met. [188]

Chinese parents recognized this social need and felt that these parties were an acceptable activity even though their teen-agers would be out late at night and miles away from home. Most parents felt their teen-agers could meet and socialize with other Chinese youth with reasonable assurance that there would be some "safety in numbers" at these large gatherings.

Chinese parents also approved of these dances because they wanted their children to have social ties with other Chinese to ensure that they would eventually marry a Chinese. They felt that if their children married other Chinese, it would help preserve Chinese traditions and values and also avoid confrontations with the white power structure. Some parents engaged in behind the scenes attempts at "match-making."

As noted in a previous chapter, some Chinese men did not go back to China to marry but formed sexual liaisons and marriages with black women. These arrangements presented problems for the Delta Chinese. Whites had gradually became more accepting of Chinese, but remained wary and critical about Chinese-black marriages. Children born of Chinese-black couples were generally unaccepted by both white and Chinese. Leaders in Chinese communities applied pressure to discourage black-Chinese marriages because they felt these liaisons harmed the

---

[188] Mae Wing, Interview, March 1, 2000.

acceptance in white society of all Chinese, as noted in this 1940 observation by an influential Southern writer.[189]

> To this end they are insisting that their men shall refrain from having Negro mistresses, and no half-breed children. When they feel that they can prove to the satisfaction of the white community that the children whom they present for admittance to the white schools are racially pure Chinese, they may attempt to have the statute repealed. If they succeed, no people will have arrived at equal opportunities for education through stranger means.

Delta Chinese Marriage Patterns

Most young Delta Chinese, not surprisingly, married other Chinese from nearby areas and typically they all came from other grocery families. The circumstances that led eventually to the marriage of John Quon and Frieda Seu were fairly representative. In Frieda Quon's words:

> I met John Quon the summer before college; we were freshmen at Ole Miss along with a lot of other Chinese students – probably the largest group of American Born Chinese (ABCs) at Ole Miss ever. That fall the Chinese freshmen had a blast, some getting academic probation. The Chinese were all majoring in engineering and pharmacy requiring tough chemistry classes difficult to pass without studying. The boys played cards, went to the movies, bowled all night, drove to Clarksdale for hot out-of-the-oven Wonder Bread. After probation, most everybody straightened up and added studying to their schedule. John changed his major from engineering to accounting, for which he was more suited. John or J.P. as he was known at college was one of the few who had a car on campus; he went home every weekend to work, so if I needed a ride home he obliged.[190]

---

[189] David L. Cohen. *Where I was Born and Raised.*

[190] Frieda Quon, Interview, Jan.12, 2000.

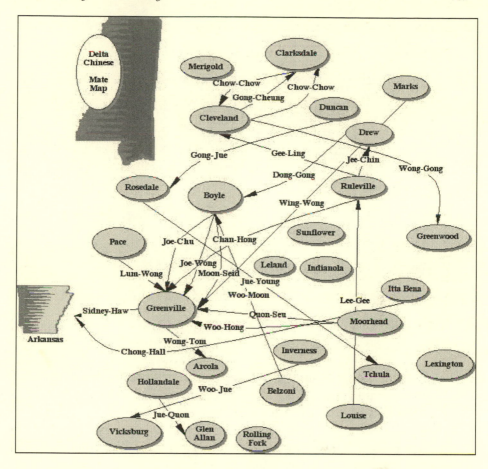

Figure 45 Sample of the marriages of Delta Chinese with others from the region from about 1950-1975. Names on each arrow are the husband-wife of each marriage, and the arrow points from each husband's hometown to his wife's hometown..

Figure 45 is by no means a complete record of marriages among Chinese from the Delta. However, it provides a visual depiction of the great extent to which young Chinese men and women from Delta towns found their marriage partners from other Delta towns. This close-knit network creates strong bonds and allegiances among the Chinese of the region.

The extent of such unions between children of other Chinese grocery families should hardly be surprising given that most young people had little opportunity to meet Chinese in other parts of the country and interracial marriages were frowned upon by Chinese as well as by whites.

A few Chinese married Chinese from outside the delta region from places like Texas, Georgia, and California. One woman, born in Brooklyn, returned to China with family, and then returned for an arranged marriage match with a Delta Chinese.

Preserving Chinese Customs

Chinese New Year festivities included shooting firecrackers and having banquet dinners with Chinese delicacies, but there were too few Chinese to have the elaborate parades with lion and dragon dances typically staged by communities with Chinatowns. Adults gave children red envelopes, *lai see*, containing monetary gifts on this and other special occasions.

> We didn't worry a lot about getting (discrimination) or people discriminating against us. We were always just told you just need to do twenty or twenty-five percent better than anybody else to get to the same place. That was a given. It wasn't something that we dwelled on. It wasn't something that we groaned about. We just knew that we needed to be twenty percent better. So that was just a go. We just did it. I think it was something I know my parents…our parents emphasized it a lot. You just got to remember you have a handicap. You are just going to have to over come it…I guess you can say it was part of the culture that you would have to leave each generation better. That was your charge. That is what Dad used to say __ you owe me. You owe me to be better than I was. My grandchildren will be better than you are.[191]

Wedding Rituals and Customs

---

[191] Juanita Dong, Interview, May 1, 2000.

Chinese weddings in the Delta dropped some aspects of traditional practices but retained others. For example, young men from her village do not carry the bride in a red sedan chair to the village of the groom, as in China. After the wedding ceremony, the bride changes from her white wedding gown to a traditional red embroidered Chinese style silk cheongsam dress. A lavish dinner with Chinese delicacies is provided for all the family and friends, many who have come from all over the country. But, before the dinner begins, a traditional tea ceremony is still observed. She and the bridegroom honor their relatives by serving tea to them.

> It's where the couple, primarily the bride, shows obedience to the groom and the groom's family. And now we have expanded where both the groom, as in my son's case_ where both the groom and the bride serve tea to both sides of the family. But in the old days, the obligation of the bride is to her in-laws because she has now become the ward of her husband's family. And that goes back to a thought of Chinese that in inheritance the wealth of the family is not usually passed on to the daughters. That's in the old custom because, again, they relied on their daughter's marrying a husband whose family is well off. Therefore she does not need to share in the wealth of her family…And, of course, this is the time that I guess, is where the mother-in-law establishes her presence. [192]

---

[192] John Paul Quon, Interview, Dec. 2, 1999.

Figure 46 The wedding banquet of John and Frieda Quon. Courtesy of Frieda Quon

If a couple decided to get married…then they would do the traditional wedding just like we would. Then afterwards they would perform the Chinese traditions. One would be the ceremony where the bride of the groom served the elders. In Chinese families, you recognized the elders as being the older. Like here is where the wisdom is and all of that. The bride and groom served tea to the elders. That would be the grandparents, parents, uncles, and aunts. In return the couple received…it could be jewelry. It could be…this is a Chinese term, *lay see*, which is a red envelope, which contains money.

Really that was the fun part. You would serve them tea. Then they would give you jewelry. It could be diamonds, pearls, gold, silver, or whatever. All the time the bride would be covered up with jewelry. It was just customary. She could even put on jewelry her mother had given her. Whatever all she had, then everything that all the people had given her. Afterwards she would go out, and everybody would just admire all the good fortune the bride had gotten. Generally it is a traditional wedding. Then sometimes there is the Tea

Ceremony. It is recognizing the elders. Then there is wishing the couple good luck. Then giving them a good start. Then usually there is a banquet. This used to be more prevalent than it is now because way back there was a lot of people who could cook. They would have these huge woks. They would be huge. They would be outside. You would have these butane burners. They could stir up a meal for hundreds of people.[193]

Ted Shepherd, the Greenville minister who presided over many Chinese weddings, explained the significant role of weddings in bringing family and friends together from all over the Delta, and beyond.

As parents save money for years just so their son or daughter can have the most scrumptious wedding that anybody could have. I have seen the auditorium full in the First Baptist Church. Some of the largest weddings we have ever had have been Chinese. They usually have those on Sunday afternoon. The reason being that all of the people that they are going to invite can close their stores on Sunday and come. They come locally...They came from Calgary, Canada and San Francisco, Seattle, Washington, Texas, and then I have had weddings where they come from Hawaii. It is a big deal.

...after the wedding she (the bride) changes into a flaming red full-length dress usually embroidered with a gold dragon on it. She will have the families of both sides giving her family jewelry. Now she can't get all on her arms and her necks so she puts it on her ankles and everywhere just diamonds and pearls, jade, and gold just hanging all over her.

She wears that at the reception in this flaming red dress... They have a very elaborate entrance. Sometimes they would have a trumpet fanfare, or a band that they have hired playing and the whole wedding party would march in... I have not said this, but family...that was the big thing with Chinese. Everything is centered on the family. It means so much to

---

[193] Frieda Quon, Interview, Jan. 12, 2000.

them. They include all of the family and everything. They do this with birthday parties. They do it with weddings, anniversaries, and all of that. Those things are very important to them.[194]

Birth Customs

After giving birth, a mother is expected to observe a month of confinement to bed. Cold, wind, dirty air, and fatigue during this period are thought to harm her in later life. She should not eat food that is "cold" (yin), thought to be unhealthy as she needs foods providing "warmth" (yang) to help her regain strength.

When new babies reached 100 days of age, traditional red egg and ginger parties were held to celebrate their entry to the community. Guests receive red dyed, hard-boiled eggs and ginger. The eggs symbolize fertility and harmony; the red color signifies good luck and a happy life. Ginger represents "hot" which has health restorative powers for the mother, weakened from childbirth. On these significant symbolic occasions, boys receive gifts of money in red envelopes and girls might get jade or gold jewelry from parents, relatives, and friends.

Celebrating Birthdays of the Elderly

Chinese, with their deep respect and veneration for elders, consider the 60th birthday, and those of every following tenth year, to be very important milestones in life. They are occasions for big celebrations to honor the person with a gathering of friends and family.

Funeral Customs

Ted Shepherd, as pastor in the Greenville Chinese Baptist Church, also presided over as many as 60 funerals. He described some of the

[194] Ted Shepherd. *The Chinese of Greenville.*

traditions and funeral customs that Chinese maintained in mourning their losses:

> Now a funeral with Chinese is another very important thing. Now when Americans die we speed things up, don't we? Yeah, we want to get our loved ones buried and get all the family in here and get it over with.
>
> They don't do that. Everything slows down. There is a week to two weeks, it doesn't matter. If they can get the whole family in here and it takes two weeks to do it then they will have the funeral then. It is usually on a Sunday afternoon so they can close all their stores, and everybody can come... if it is a very well known or prominent Chinese they will have it at First Baptist Church...
>
> After a Chinese funeral they have a meal for everyone that attends. If there was a thousand people, you were invited. They have a Chinese food for them. Usually on a wedding it is a nine-course meal of Chinese food. They don't serve quite that much at a Chinese funeral. It would be five or six courses. They have the soup and the rice and the fish dishes and the meat and the duck and all of that. Everybody was invited. Now most of the family will wear black, and the pallbearers will wear white gloves. Sometimes arm bands for every family member, cousins, little bitty baby, everybody would get a black armband.
>
> Funeral customs involve bringing the hearse back past the home of the deceased after the church funeral service before making the journey to the cemetery. All mourners receive a red envelope, lai see, containing a nickel and a piece of candy to provide sweetness to help deal with the bitter sorrow.[195]

---

[195] Ibid.

Figure 47 Chinese cemetery, Greenville, Ms. Courtesy of Ted Shepherd

As noted by John Paul Quon:

And that basically indicates that the people that attended will be more prosperous and they will have no bitterness in their mouth. So there is some symbolism there. And then after that the family will revisit the grave three days later. It is automatically three days later. So the funeral process can extend beyond a week. If somebody dies on a weekday, the funeral is usually going to be on Sunday so all of the Chinese can attend.

...Respecting the elders. And one sign of respecting the elders, especially the deceased, at Easter time traditionally there are some similarities with the Christian ceremony [in] that they place flowers at the grave. And many Chinese do. But then there are some Chinese that will prepare a full-course meal and take it out to the gravesite and even place the place setting at the grave. And then the family will sit there and share that meal and at the site. So that is still a custom that some Chinese do practice, especially at the Greenville Chinese cemetery. I can't give an explanation. I always look at it on the humorous side that Chinese rather eat than sniff roses or flowers. So we're a lot more practical from that viewpoint.[196]

In China each spring families pay respect to ancestors and recently deceased relatives by gathering at the cemetery to clean and decorate the gravesites. In addition to food offerings, they may burn incense sticks, joss sticks, paper money, and paper clothing in the belief that relatives can receive even money if it is burned. This ancient ceremony, Ching Ming, was practiced in the Delta by the early Chinese, but not to the extent as in China. The custom is part of the traditional value that Chinese place on honoring elders.

> But speaking of elders, I think that probably the whole society or the social structure is based on elders. If you will go into a Chinese home, there will always be a picture of the parents, the immediate parents on display, the deceased father and deceased mother that will be on display in some form or fashion. In a way, it pays homage to them, but it's not quite paganistic. But yet, they're there. And then if they are alive, they are always, always treated well. There are many Chinese that are infirm, but they very seldom go to a nursing home because the family has considered it as their responsibility to maintain their elders.[197]

Because white cemeteries would not accept burial of Chinese, the Delta Chinese built their own cemetery in 1913. But with passing years they needed more space and built a larger one on 5.8 acres of land acquired for $1,000 in 1931. A pagoda similar to those found at cemeteries in China graces the entrance (See Figure 47). Although located in Greenville, many Chinese immigrants in towns as distant as Belzoni,

---

[196] John Paul Quon, Interview, Dec. 2, 1999.
[197] Ibid.

Hollandale, and Indianola wanted to be interred there upon death.[198] This preference for their final resting place is one further example of their strong sense of Chinese identity.

Generational Clash of Cultural Values

As each successive cohort of American-born Chinese became increasingly assimilated to American values, it is not surprising that they began to challenge, or at least question, the usefulness of some of the traditions and values their parents brought from the old country.

The expected filial piety and obedience of the children to the wishes of authoritarian fathers were at odds with the American ideals of individualism and personal choice that they learned in school. In the traditional Chinese family, fathers expected their children to follow their wishes unquestioningly. Children who did not comply often faced physical punishment. Two examples illustrate the disciplinary power that fathers had on their children. A father punished his son with a few swipes from a stick to his rear end on one occasion because he disapproved of his playing with black children. Another time when his son accepted a free snow cone from a customer, the father similarly punished him because he did not believe children should accept gifts from other people they did not know well.[199] A young daughter sent temporarily to live with her grandparents defiantly refused to attend school but after her father spoke to her on the telephone, she immediately relented. When she had to have her tonsils removed, she stubbornly refused to cooperate with the procedures. However, once her father appeared on the scene, she quickly

---

[198] Ted Shepherd.,*The Chinese of Greenville*. 46-54.
[199] Raymond Wong, Interview by John Jung, Sept. 13, 2008.

complied. In both instances, she obeyed the authority of the father, without the need for any punishment.[200]

As they became more Americanized, the children began to question the authority of the father and other values of the Chinese family even though they appreciated their parents' hard work and efforts in providing for them. Not fully aware of the social conditions that their parents had suffered under and the sacrifices their parents had made, second-and later generation Chinese often failed to see the vital role that family life served for the Chinese immigrants in America. In many respects, the family was a refuge for the immigrants from the prejudices and unfair society in which they had to struggle. In contrast, their American-born children often experienced the traditional Chinese family structure and values as a burden for them.

Although her interviews of Chinese Americans were from the Los Angeles area around 1931, Lei Jieqiong's Master's thesis painted a dismal view of their situation that was valid for American-born Chinese throughout the United States for several decades. Among her conclusions as summarized by a reviewer:[201]

> Social segregation, discrimination, and identity crisis were some of the major problems they were confronted with. Though born and raised in the United States, they felt far less secure about their future and far less confident about their identity than the immigrant generation...

---

[200] Blanche Yee, Interview, Sept. 14, 2008.

[201] Haiming Lui (May 2007). "The Identity Formation of American-Born Chinese in the 1930s: A Review of Lei Jieqiong's (Kit King Louis) Master's Thesis." *Journal Of Chinese Overseas 3*, 1: 97–121.

In the eyes of American-born Chinese, however, home was the first obstacle to achieving full assimilation. The more they grew up, the more uncomfortable they became about the differences between Chinese culture and mainstream American culture. The Chinese home was like a meeting ground where two cultures clashed. While immigrant parents followed Chinese traditions, spoke the Cantonese dialect and acted as if they were still in China, the second generation resented parental control, disparaged the Chinese life style, and saw themselves as Americans.

Parents, on the other hand, did not value or welcome many of the American ways that their children were embracing. Participation in American athletic sports such as football, for example, represented an valued goal for male adolescents who wanted to be part of American society. However, such pursuits were not valued by the early immigrant generations. Their children had to fight the prejudices of white coaches and teammates that blocked their acceptance in athletics as well as opposition at home from parents who disapproved of such activities.[202]

However, eventually Chinese Americans did break through these barriers, and became accepted and successful in these activities. As the newspaper clipping in Figure 48 shows, several Joe Brothers in Boyle were among the first Chinese to achieve recognition in high school athletics.

Career choices also could be a source of conflict between parents and children. Chinese wanted their children to be financially successful. They favored their sons entering into practical and lucrative careers in accounting, business, pharmacy, medicine, or engineering, for example.

---

[202] "I had to beg grandma let me stay in sports because my dad will not let me." e-mail to Author, Robert Chow, March 27, 2008.

Fields such as art, music, interior decoration, journalism, or counseling were discouraged as impractical and poor ways to earn a living.

Figure 48 Several Delta Chinese including several Joe brothers (Walter, Peter, Ed, and Fee) and Charlie Chu were local high school football players.

Girls were not encouraged to pursue higher education or careers as it was hoped that they would marry a successful man and focus on raising a family. But with the incorporation of American values that encouraged pursuit of one's dreams and developing one's talents, the career choices of children did not always match those favored by parents. Social changes during the 1960s and later opened opportunities for women and led many daughters to obtain higher education and pursue careers rather than accept the traditional stay-at-home mom role.

A matter of even greater concern to Chinese parents was interracial dating because it might lead to mixed marriages. As previously mentioned, the immigrant generation wanted their American-born children to meet and eventually marry Chinese. As long as racial segregation and traditions were firmly in place, the issue was not a real concern because even if Chinese youth wanted to date non-Chinese, they would likely be rejected. After World War II, social barriers between races began to weaken and more Chinese families faced conflicts as interracial dating increased. Some entered into interracial marriages, and in some cases, had mixed race children.

> The old argument used by parents__ "you should be Chinese because you won't be accepted as a Caucasian anyway"__ is losing its force, as the children are beginning to be accepted.[203]

However, the increasingly more open society and more accepting attitudes about mixed race marriages combined with the limited number of eligible Chinese mates increased the likelihood that Chinese would socialize with, date, and marry Caucasians.

> "I didn't go to the Chinese dances. My parents tried to push us to go, and we resented it…I mostly know Caucasians. They were my friends, the only people I know."…On the other hand, those who do attend Chinese functions also express ambivalence about their participation and their Chinese heritage. Most Chinese young people, for example, are not really proud of their ability to speak two languages and have made no effort to learn written Chinese.[204]

---

[203] James Loewen. *The Mississippi Chinese*, 160.
[204] Ibid., 160.

There is a bit of irony that as the Chinese, once denied access to white schools, hospitals, neighborhoods, and other desirable places, began to face a disintegration or loss of many Chinese customs and values at the same time they gained in social status and privilege. For the immigrant generation, white acceptance came at a price. Increased acculturation of their children to white values occurred and, not surprisingly, it led to more out-marriages. Over time, as more mixed-race marriages occurred, parents found it easier to acknowledge this reality. They began to realize that it was more important that their children have a good marriage rather than to worry about the race of the mates that their children chose. Unlike in the past, their children also gained greater freedom and opportunities in many other important aspects of life. Those changes reflected real progress for Chinese and other ethnic minorities.

10. Legacy of Delta Chinese Grocery Stores

Children of immigrants are often referred to as the "second generation," but this term does not adequately distinguish between distinct cohorts of children of immigrants born in different eras. When children of immigrants born in different decades are lumped together as "second generation" it overlooks the fact that the social conditions in which these different cohorts grew up were quite different and had different consequences. "Second-generation" Chinese varied also in whether they were born in China or in the U. S. Further complicating classifications, depending on their year of birth, some third or later generation children experienced conditions more similar to those of the early immigrants than some second-generation children faced. For example, a third-generation Chinese born before 1920 would have encountered more racial prejudice than a second-generation Chinese born, say, after 1940. Perhaps a more useful grouping might be to combine children that, regardless of generation or U.S. versus China birthplace, grew up in Delta Chinese grocery stores and compare them with children that did not have this background.

The legacy of grocery parents for their children was both material and cultural. Some children from the cohort born in the 1920s and 1930s inherited the grocery stores when their parents retired or died. For many at that time, this was a valuable legacy as there were few options for young Chinese because racial discrimination limited employment opportunities. Even if they had the education and training that qualified them for professions, discrimination denied them access. This situation was not limited to the Delta but existed throughout North America for Chinese Americans born in the late 1920s and early 1930s. Chinese American writers like Jade Snow Wong[205] and Pardee Lowe[206] broke new ground by writing about being denied opportunities by racial prejudice against Chinese even though they had college degrees, spoke proficient English, and were highly assimilated.

In addition, the second generation carried the work ethic, moral values, and Chinese world-view that their parents had imparted to them. This cultural legacy proved to be both a blessing and a burden. On the positive side, it served to unify Chinese in the Delta and provided attitudes toward life that served them well throughout their lives.

However, American-born children, and those who came over at an early age, grew up learning and valuing American customs and attitudes as well as those they learned at home from their parents. The American and Chinese cultural values clashed at times, creating confusion for the children and conflict between the parents and children. At times the children felt embarrassed by the Chinese ways of their parents and insecure about meeting white standards. The assimilation of the children to American ways while their parents tried to inculcate Chinese customs and culture was stressful for both parties.

As Randy Kwan who grew up in Greenville during the turbulent 1960s reflected about his feelings of ethnic identity conflict and confusion:

> Growing up in the Mississippi Delta in the seventies was very confusing...As a child of an immigrant Chinese

---

[205] Jade Snow Wong. *Fifth Chinese Daughter.*
[206] Pardee Lowe. *Father and Glorious Descendant.*

father and a second generation Chinese mother, I was exposed to a clash of cultural mores and social etiquette that I did not fully grasp until I went to college and then moved away from Mississippi.

Like Chinese fried rice, my cultural experience was a mixture of various leftovers from the previous era of social segregation. By birth, I was Chinese and was taught about the 3,300 year-old culture of the homeland of my parents and relatives. By heritage, we were not fully accepted by the post Civil Rights integration imposed on Southern society by the federal government. I was also aware that I would have to conform to the predominant culture of the time in order to be successful. By circumstance, I was knowledgeable and felt comfortable weaving in and out of rural Mississippi Black culture since the majority of Chinese businesses thrived in the black areas of small towns and cities across the South.

During the early seventies, there were no lasting Chinese role models in America. Mass media upheld the White culture as role models. Blacks were gaining power in the media and were exercising their influence in feature films, television, and print media…The lack of an Asian role model made me very insecure about my social worth since it was obvious I did not truly fit into the American ideal… My hair was black…My eyes were dark brown and slanted versus blue or green. I did not have a large physique that made African Americans imposing on the movie or television screen. The only Asians seen in the media were Hop Sing, the cook on Bonanza, or the stereotypical evil mystical character from a distant shore that could kill a person with a single touch…[207]

His identity conflicts were, of course, not unique to Chinese growing up during these years in the Delta but were felt by Chinese all

---

[207] Roderick Randell Kwan, Comments Jan. 11, 2007.

over the U. S. Despite the exposure to many books on Chinese history and culture provided by his parents and the viewing of numerous PBS documentaries that proclaimed the rich heritage of Chinese culture, Randy still experienced a lack of connection to Chinese heritage.

Eventually his professional work as a film and television cameraman took him to China and his experiences there began to help him put all the pieces of his identity together. He observed, "I finally stood in the land of my father, proud to be whom I am: Chinese, American, and Southern."[208]

Many Delta Chinese hold similar strong identification with the region as voiced by Penney Gong who explained:

> I have always enjoyed it here. I call myself a true southerner. I have grown up here. I have never wanted to move away.[209]

These sentiments resemble those expressed by Sung Gay Chow, who no longer lives in the Delta. His views demonstrate that identity clearly involves much more than ethnicity:

> The majority of us feel like we are part of the South. We speak the same language—i.e. dialect—and we hold the same likes, dislikes, and values that so many southerners hold. Many Chinese Americans left the Delta for jobs and economic reasons and not necessarily because they hated Mississippi. I think most of them still have affection for the Delta__it's their home. We might disagree with the South in general or Mississippi in particular on a number of issues, but we still get defensive, especially when other parts of the country badmouth us. It's kind of hard to explain, but it's something like this: You might have a serious disagreement

---

[208] Ibid.

[209] Penney Gong, Interview, Oct. 7, 1999.

with your brother and get into a fight and not speak to each other for a while, but if anyone outside the family says something negative about your brother, you're going to defend him.[210]

It is easy to overlook the existence of a regional influence on the way Chinese Americans live and think because the majority live near the east or the west coast. Yet no one would make the mistake of equating white Southerners with white Northerners in outlook and lifestyles. Similarly, "Southern" Chinese Americans are not the same as those in other parts of the country. While all Chinese Americans of a generation hold in common many Chinese values and perspectives, those in the South diverge from their counterparts in other regions in many dimensions. Whites, blacks, and Chinese, despite their differences, still share a "regional identity." As Southerners, they proudly see themselves as more informal, conservative, patriotic, involved with fundamental religion, and friendlier than people from other regions.

Conclusion

Children of grocers from cohorts born during and after WWII in the 1940s and 1950s had far wider educational, social, and economic opportunities than earlier cohorts. They came of age after the 1960s, which saw the rapid expansion of civil rights for minorities. By the last quarter of the twentieth century, many of the children of the Chinese grocers born between the Great Depression and the end of World War II, with the urging and support of their parents attended colleges and universities in the South, and elsewhere. Many achieved distinction, with large percentages creating successful careers in many professions,

---

[210] Sung Gay Chow, e-mails to Author, September 1, 2008., October 5, 2008

including engineering, pharmacy, medicine, accounting, the arts, and computer technology, to name a few. No longer were educated Chinese restricted to a future in the grocery business. Many left the region to seek and accept employment in professional careers that are more plentiful outside of the Delta, in other areas of the South, and beyond.

Cohort differences among second, and later generations, also existed with respect to the ethnic background of marriage partners. Whereas almost all of the children of the cohort born in the 1920s and the 1930s married other Chinese, both due to parental wishes and partly due to a segregated society, increased rates of out-marriage occurred, mostly to white partners, reflecting the changes in social attitudes toward Chinese as they improved their status in society over succeeding decades. Such out-marriages would have been highly unacceptable to most Chinese parents before the 1960s. They no longer encounter much, if any, opposition from parents. While most Chinese parents still preferred that their children marry other Chinese, they adjusted and learned to embrace their non-Chinese daughters- and sons-in law.

It was clear by these developments that the future for the Chinese community was rapidly changing.[211] As Robert Seto Quon wrote in *Lotus Among the Magnolias*, parents resigned themselves to the inevitable departure of their children from the Delta. He noted that one mother acknowledged, "They got to leave because their professions demand it. If there were better opportunities here they might stay, but there ain't. We

---

[211] James L. Loewen, "The Mississippi Chinese."

older people know that. And they want more freedom now. The Delta's too small for them."[212]

On the assumption that the future would not bring many new Chinese immigrants to the Delta, Quan predicted that the exodus of many of the young adult generation would lead the Chinese Delta community membership to disperse.[213] This forecast made a quarter of a century ago certainly seems supported now near the end of the first decade of the 21st century. James Loewen, a highly respected observer of the Delta Chinese reiterated the same prognosis he had made as early as 1971.[214]

> The young people are also continuing to leave. One propellant continues to be their desire to evade their ambiguous racial status in the Delta, while another is their wish to escape the limitations of being Chinese in the Delta.

While newer Chinese immigrants have come to the region since the 1965 liberalization of immigration laws, many of them came with more education and financial resources than the pioneers from Guangdong did a century ago. But the descendants of these Chinese from Guangdong still living in the Delta are few and their numbers continue to decline.

Many aspects of life in the Delta have changed significantly, and often for the worse, over the past generation. Such adverse conditions are by no means limited to young Chinese Americans. Since the Great Depression, cotton production has become entirely mechanized. Even so, cotton has not been very profitable, as competition from other countries has increased, leaving the region highly dependent on federal agricultural

---

[212] Robert Seto Quan, *Lotus Among the Magnolias,* 153.
[213] Ibid.
[214] James W. Loewen, *The Mississippi Chinese,* 198.

subsidies. The cotton plantations that once dominated the Delta economy when the Chinese first opened their groceries have long since faded into history.

The civil rights activism of the 1950s and 1960s produced long overdue changes to remedy past inequities and injustices in the social fabric of race relations in the Delta. These changes redefined many aspects of Delta life, including the role of the grocery business for Chinese Americans, as noted earlier.

The overall economy in the Delta has been in a tailspin for decades, occasionally boosted by the arrival of some industry such as carpet mills and manufacturing of towboats, but their benefits are often temporary. Throughout the Delta, people of all backgrounds have moved away due to the loss of jobs with the closure of many manufacturing plants. Those who remain face increased crime, violence, youth gangs, and drugs that destroy the communities.

In this environment, Chinese grocery stores have dwindled to only a few and they are faced with strong competition from super market chains. The children of the grocers, armed with their college educations, hold bright hopes for professional careers. They can hardly be faulted for having no interest in operating their parents' grocery stores, businesses that ironically financed their freedom. The breakdown of many barriers in Delta society against Chinese in the past now affords them far wider opportunities, professional and personal, than could have been dreamed possible a generation ago. The younger generations of Chinese are also increasingly exercising their freedom to marry someone other than another Chinese, if they are so inclined.

The Chinese that grew up in the groceries managed to straddle, and successfully negotiate two worlds, that of their immigrant parents and that of the host culture of the Delta. But their own children, those of the third, fourth, and later generations did not face this task. Many attended private mostly white schools, lived in middle class white neighborhoods, and socialized with mostly whites. For these generations, the legacy of the grocery store is not as readily apparent. Perhaps, once they acquire an interest in and study the history of Chinese in the Delta, they will recognize and claim their legacy.

Chinese that did come from the grocery stores agree in seeing a bleak future for their children in the Delta, as illustrated by this sample of observations.

> Yeah I agree. I don't think there is any future for the kids being educated here unless you can find a job around here. I don't think there is that much opportunity here. When we came, I think we were one of the first Chinese families here. There were fifty Chinese here then and seven grocery stores. Now there is only one grocery store. There is only six Chinese.

> Everybody else is moving to Texas, California. We have a kid in Illinois. We have one in Texas. Then we have a boy that is supposed to graduate this year. Then our daughter… that is at L. S. U. … In fact before we closed the store, we asked our youngest boy. Well, we ask them all, the youngest boy especially, because he was the playboy in the family. He went to Mississippi State …the first year, he got a $4000 scholarship from Mississippi State. He played around. He had a .5 average. So we pulled him out, and we sent him to Delta State. His grades improved (a little) … so we pulled him out of there. He got mad… so he went to work for about six months before he went back to school. We told him that he needed to go back to school. So that put him about a year

and half__ almost two years__ behind. He went back to school. Now he is kind of matured. We offered him the store first. The oldest one, and he said he didn't want it. We ask him if he wanted to run the store. He said if he ran the store in two years he would be out of business. So we decided to sell it. If he didn't want to run it, and we had the opportunity...so we sold it. He said that he didn't want to come back to Hollandale.

Nobody wants to come back to Hollandale or to Mississippi because they say nothing is here. He is going to school at Southern Mississippi. Priscilla is still kind of a small town. It is not what you would call a big town. He said coming to Hollandale, it is just like it is dead. Our younger daughter is even worse. She goes to school at L. S. U. in Baton Rouge. She said there is so much to do there. She said after two days of coming home, she is ready to go back to school.

I don't see them coming back to the Mississippi Delta. I think (of) the original Chinese of the Mississippi Delta. They are almost extinct... After our generation leaves, I think it is history. I think we need to preserve history now... so many things have changed since the fifties and sixties. Our kids have become Americanized, and they are blended in with society ... just don't want the life that we led. In which you cannot blame them ... you know... eighty hours a week, you don't get any enjoyment. You can't do anything. You see the future for the younger kids. For them to come back to the Delta or Mississippi itself, the only place I see them going is probably Jackson. They might go to the Gulf Coast, I don't see that much on the Gulf Coast. If they come back, they'd probably would go to Jackson where the factories are and the jobs are. If you are an engineer with M. C. I. World, some company like that... they might come back. I don't see them coming back to the Delta. [215]

---

[215] Bobby and Laura Jue, Interview, Feb. 4, 2000.

His wife concurred by noting that:

I think the younger generation is going to go off because they
have to go to the big cities to find a job. My generation, they
have had a lot more people stay in Delta because they have
their own store. They have their own business. They can
raise the family. Our children…when they finish school, they
will move somewhere else. I don't think they will come back
here to raise their family. I think there will be less and less
Chinese. We are retired right now. We might spend the rest
of our life here, or we might move somewhere else. I am not
sure yet. I have got to wait until the children see where they
can move. We never know that until that many years later. I
have been living in Mississippi. I am glad we sold the store.
We closed the store. I thought I would move off somewhere
else, but after a few months of thinking about it. I have been
living here for thirty years. I have friends here. I have got
used to the country life. When I drive, we don't have a far
stretch. It is not that many cars. The traffic is not that heavy.
216

We have raised our three children here. I have three children,
two daughters and a son. All three of them, two of my
daughters have graduated from Delta State, have very good
jobs. My son is a junior this year. They never thought of
going anywhere else. Delta State is the only school they ever
wanted to go to. It has set a good background for what they
are doing now. My daughter moved to Oregon, and she lived
there for three years. She has come home to Mississippi
because she feels more comfortable here. She enjoyed being
in Oregon, but this is home. [217]

---

[216] Ibid.
[217] Penny Gong, Interview, Oct. 7, 1999.

Figure 49 Top row: Two Greenville stores in their prime in the 1940s: Mee Jon Grocery (left) Courtesy, Sidney family and Joe Gow Nue No. 2 (right) Courtesy, Dicksun Joe. Bottom row: Same buildings in empty decay in 2008. Courtesy, Blanche and Bill Yee.

As illustrated in Figure 49 by the physical decay of two of the few still standing buildings in the Delta that once contained thriving grocery stores, the Chinese grocery store is now fast fading into history, just as the old cotton plantation became obsolete, and there is no hope or reason for the family grocery store to continue to be viable in the future. In its time, it served a critical role in the history of Delta Chinese. The grocery store provided a unique opportunity for the early Chinese to earn a living, although a difficult one, that allowed them and their families to forge successful lives despite tremendous odds against them. In fact, it was probably the only avenue for them to become entrepreneurs as most other opportunities were denied to them prior to the end of the Jim Crow era in the South. This niche fulfilled the same economic role that the hand laundry, and eventually the family restaurant, had for early Chinese immigrants in most parts of the country other than the Delta, which was one of the few exceptions in not having Chinese laundries. Through these family-owned and operated stores, these hardy, courageous, resourceful, and industrious families persevered despite racial and economic obstacles to emerge victorious.

One additional stark reminder of the end of an era is the fate of the small Chinese Baptist Church in Cleveland. By 2000, the dozen or so worshippers attending the Sunday services were the among the rapidly declining numbers from the ranks of Chinese grocers and their families that built their own church in the days when white churches excluded them.[218] In its day, the Chinese Mission school, which it operated, served as an invaluable community resource for the Chinese but the combination of improved societal attitudes toward the Chinese and the decline in Chinese grocery stores over the years reduced the number of Chinese in the region finding it necessary. Having fulfilled its purpose and outlived its need, the long vacant Chinese Mission School building in Cleveland, Mississippi was demolished in 2003.

The story of the Chinese grocers in the Delta for over a century is noteworthy because of its unique circumstances. For unlike the Chinese who settled in cities like San Francisco, Chicago, or New York with

---

[218] Somini Sengupta. "Delta Chinese Hang On to a Vanishing Way of Life." *Cleveland Journal,* November 1, 2000.

"Chinatowns," which provided them with the familiarity and comfort afforded by daily and easy access to Chinese commodities, customs, and companionship, the Chinese in the Delta lived in a diffuse sprawling "community" that stretched for over a hundred and fifty miles north and south and fifty miles east and west. Most of the people they lived around were black or white, and they did not exactly welcome the Chinese into the region. Such circumstances compelled the few and scattered Chinese of the Delta to develop strong network ties among themselves that were probably stronger than those among the thousands of Chinese confined to ethnic enclaves in metropolitan areas.

Although often suffering unfair treatment, the Delta Chinese pioneers did not unduly concern themselves about these inequities. Instead, they directed their energies toward improving their own station in life. Realizing they were far outnumbered and lacking in political power and social status, they set about changing the things they felt they had some influence rather than dwelling on the conditions that were beyond their control. Through their grocery stores, they earned their living through thrift, discipline, business acumen, and resilience. The Chinese grocers were committed to providing their children with the financial means to gain college educations so they could enjoy a better station in life.

Chinese immigrants and their families not only provided for their own interests but at the same time they:

> …have made invaluable contributions to the quality of life in the Delta, serving as town mayors, leaders of civic clubs and churches, and in all facets of community life in the Delta. Their stores and businesses have played an important role in

the Delta economy. Their commitment to educational excellence has been a model for all the citizens of the Delta.[219]

Despite the prejudices and mistreatment that the Chinese endured for many years, they found a way to emerge with a fierce loyalty and devotion to the Delta. Most of those who left the region for economic and professional reasons held no bitterness or resentment. The strong allegiances to the region and social bonds formed with each other as a close knit Delta-wide "community" prompts many expatriates to return to the Delta on many occasions including reunions, marriages of their children, births of grandchildren, and funerals of their parents and older relatives. Some have even returned to retire in the Delta.

A Delta-wide Chinese community "reunion" known as the "Big Event" held in 1987 amply illustrates the strength of Mississippi roots among the Chinese who grew up in the region. Over 500 Chinese, and their families, from all over the United States converged in Greenville for a unprecedented weekend gathering to renew acquaintances with each other. The brainchild of Greenville resident, Raymond Wong, it provided a rare opportunity for the Chinese from the region to demonstrate their strong emotional ties to the region and to their fellow Chinese from grocery store families. The front cover of the commemorative album created for the Big Event is shown below in Figure 50.

---

[219] John Thornell (2008). "A Culture in Decline: The Chinese in the Mississippi Delta." *Southeast Asian Review*, 30, 196-202.

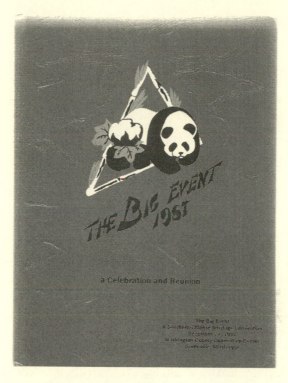

Figure 50 Commemerative album cover for the Big Event, Greenville, 1987 designed by Harry Gong.

Many of the participants had left the Delta over 30 years ago for opportunities in other parts of the country and this occasion was one of their few, if not the first, return visits to the region. It was a cause for celebration, nostalgia, and renewal of childhood friendships that were born in the Delta where they had once lived as marginal members of their communities. During this one weekend, they reflected on and rejoiced in the positive aspects of their previous years living in the Delta.

Another striking testament of the strong bonds that connect the Delta Chinese to each other is an annual Southern Chinese reunion cruise. On a smaller scale than the Big Event, this affair reunites over one hundred Delta Chinese from all over the country for a weeklong cruise of camaraderie and nostalgia. Figure 51 shows the participants in the excursion of 2005.

However, as with similar events such as high school and college reunions, participants at such gatherings are generally the more successful members of their groups. How successful were the peers who do not attend? Did they have less positive ties to their Delta roots? Despite this lack of information about those the absentees, it should in no way diminish the considerable evidence of successful life achievements among those Delta Chinese represented at this event.

In the celebratory and congratulatory atmosphere of such gatherings, however, participants should also acknowledge the struggles and hardships that their parents and grandparents had to face, the sacrifices they made, and the values they taught that provided their children with the foundation for success in life. As a Chinese proverb advises, "When you drink water, remember the source."

The history of the Delta Chinese contains many valuable lessons about how to deal with adversity, the importance of working together with family members, and the value and methods of establishing good will and harmony with both the black and white communities. Current and future generations of Chinese associated with the Delta have a positive legacy from their past that offers a firm foundation for their future success in life.

Figure 51 The 2005 Southern Chinese Reunion Cruise participants. Courtesy, Paul Wong.

Timeline of Major Events in U. S. and the Delta Affecting Chinese

Year	United States	Mississippi Delta
1849	Gold discovered in California increases Chinese immigration.	
1869	Transcontinental railroad completed in Utah and thousands of Chinese seek work elsewhere	
1870s	Anti-Chinese views and violence spreads in western states	Chinese labor recruited to South
1880s		Chinese open grocery stores throughout Delta
	1882 Chinese Exclusion Act	
1924	Immigration Act based on National Quotas	More Chinese grocers wives and children in Delta
1927		Supreme Court upholds ban of Chinese from white schools in Ms.
1930s	Great Depression and start of World War II	Chinese Mission Schools opened
1943	End of Chinese Exclusion Act	
1940s	Increased mechanization of cotton farming reduces work for labor	white schools admit Chinese late 40s, early 50s
1945	End of World War II	Improved acceptance of Chinese
1954	Supreme Court 'ends' school desegregation	
1960s		More Chinese attend college, enter professions
1965	Immigration Law reform increases entry from Asian nations	Chinese, and their groceries, reach a peak and decline
1970		Public school desegregated; private schools grow
1980s-		More decline in Chinese grocery stores; more young adults move from Delta for career opportunities

Bibliography

Adams, Jane, & D. Gorton. "Southern trauma: Revisiting caste and class in the Mississippi Delta."*American Anthropologist, 106*, 2, (2004): 334-345.

Adams, Samuel C *Changing Negro life in the Delta.* (Nashville, TN: Fisk University, 1947).

Bolton, Charles C. *The Hardest Deal of All: The Battle over School Integration in Mississippi, 1870-1980.* Jackson, Ms.: University Press of Mississippi, 2005.

Bow, Leslie. "Meditations on the partly colored." Southern Review, 43, 1, (2007): 89-95.

Brasell, R. Bruce "So that we have our own color: Mississippi Triangle, textual posturing, and racial negotiation" *Film Criticism, 2002.*

Chow, Sally. Interview by John Jung, Aug. 28, 2007.

Chow, Sung Gay "A Personal View of the Mississippi Chinese." In *Mississippi Writers: Reflections of Childhood and Youth.* Vol. II, ed. D. Abbot, 75-97. Jackson, MS: University Press of Mississippi, 1985.

Choy, Christine, Long, Worth, & Siegel, Allan. *Mississippi Triangle.* New York: Third World Newsreel, 1984.

Cohn, David L. *Where I Was Born and Raised.* Notre Dame and London: University of Notre Dame Press, 1948.

Cohen, Lucy M. *Chinese in the Post-Civil War South.* Baton Rouge: Louisiana State University, 1984.

Dollard, John. *Caste and Class in a Southern Town.* Garden City, New York: Doubleday. Sec. Ed., 1949.

Dong, Fay. Interview by Kimberly Lancaster, May 1, 2000, transcript, Delta State University Oral History Archives, Cleveland, Ms.

Dong, Juanita. Interview by Kimberly Lancaster, May 1, 2000, transcript, Delta State University Oral History Archives, Cleveland, Ms.

Fairbanks, John King, ed. *The Missionary Enterprise in China and America.* Cambridge, MA; Harvard University Press, 1974.

Gong, Penny. Interview by Georgene Clark, Oct. 7, 1999, transcript, Delta State University Oral History Archives, Cleveland, Ms.

Gong, Gwendolyn. "The changing use of deference among the Mississippi Chinese." *English Today,* 19, (2003): 50-56.

"Grocer, employee shot to death in Shaw armed robbery." Associated Press, Sept. 20, 2007.

Hen, Arlee. Interview with Judy Yung at Greenville, Mississippi, December 1982. Chinese Women of America Research Project, Chinese Culture Foundation of San Francisco.

Hong, Sherman *Growing up in the Mississippi Delta,* Unpublished, 2008.

Joe, Edward and Annette. Interview by Kimberly Lancaster and Jennifer Mitchell, May 1, 2000, transcript. Delta State University Oral History Archives, Cleveland, Ms.

Joe, Peter Y. *The Joe Family of Boyle, Mississippi.* Unpublished, 2007.

Jue. Bobby and Laura. Interview by Kimberly Lancaster, Feb. 4, 2000, transcript, Delta State University Oral History Archives, Cleveland, Ms.

Jung, John *Chinese Laundries: Tickets to Survival on Gold Mountain.* Cypress, Ca.: Yin and Yang Press, 2007.

Jung, Moon-Ho. *Coolies and cane: Race, Labor, and Sugar in the Age of Emancipation.* Baltimore, MD.: Johns Hopkins University Press, 2006.

Kung, S. W. *Chinese in American Life.* Seattle: University of Washington Press, 1962., 55.

Kwan, Roderick Randell. *Comments made at the Opening of the History of the Mississippi Delta Chinese Photo Exhibit,* Capps Archives, Delta State University, Jan. 11, 2007.

Kwan, Shirley Hong Woo "Growing Up in the Mississippi Delta." Unpublished manuscript.

Lee, Hoover. Telephone interview by John Jung, Aug. 16, 2007.

Lee, Joseph Tse-Hei. "The Overseas Chinese networks and early Baptist missionary movement across the South China sea." *Historian,* 63 (Summer 2001): 753–768.

Lew, Bonnie C "I always felt out of place there. Growing up Chinese in Mississippi." In *Chinese American Voices: From the Gold Rush to the Present,* edited by Judy Yung, Gordon H. Chang & Him Mark Lai, 281–291. Berkeley and Los Angeles, Ca.: University of California Press, 2006.

Liang, Zhou, "Life of a Chinese American Grocer in the South," *China Daily,* 1961. Nd, Zhou Liang, Translation from Chinese to English, 2001.

Liao, Pao Yun "A Case Study of a Chinese Immigrant Community." M. A. Thesis, Sociology, University of Chicago (1951): 43.

Lim de Sánchez, Sieglinde. "Crafting a Delta Chinese: Education and acculturation in twentieth-century southern Baptist mission schools." *History of Education Quarterly,* 43, 1, 2003: 74-90.

Loewen, James. W. *The Mississippi Chinese: Between Black and White.* Sec. Edition, Long Grove, Il.: Waveland Press, 1988.

Love, Ronald. Review of *Lotus Among the Magnolias: The Mississippi Chinese,* by Robert Seto Quan, in collaboration with Julian B. Roebuck. *Social Forces,* 62, 3, (1984): 832-833.

Lowe, Pardee. *Father and Glorious Descendant.* Boston, Little, Brown, 1943.

Lui, Haiming. The Identity Formation of American-Born Chinese in the 1930s: A Review of Lei Jieqiong's (Kit King Louis) Master's Thesis *Journal Of Chinese Overseas 3,* 1 (May 2007): 97–121.

McCunn, Ruthanne Lum "Arlee Hen and Black Chinese" In *Chinese American Portraits: Personal Histories 1828-1988:* 79-87. San Francisco: Chronicle Books, 1988.

Miller, Martha S. Interview by Molly Shaman, Dec. 3, 1999. transcript, Delta State University Oral History Archives, Cleveland, Ms.

Mississippi Triangle, Dir. Christine Choi, Worth Long, and Allan Siegel. New York: Third World Newsreel, 1984

Moon, Bobby Joe. *"Growing up in Mississippi in the '40s - '60s."* *http://usads.ms11.net/bjm.html. Accessed August 1, 2006.*

New York Times, "Chinese for the South." March 9, 1880, 1.

O'Brien, Robert W. "Status of Chinese in the Mississippi Delta." *Social Forces,* 19, 3 (1941): 386-390.

Percy, William Alexander. *Lanterns on the Levee: Recollections of a Planter's Son* New York: Alfred A. Knopf, 1941.

Quan, Robert Seto. *Lotus Among Magnolias: The Mississippi Chinese.* Jackson: University Press of Mississippi, 1982.

Quon. Frieda. Interview by Kimberly Lancaster and Jennifer Mitchell, Jan.12, 2000. transcript, Delta State University Oral History Archives, Cleveland, Ms.

Quon, John Paul. Interview by Margaret Tullos, Dec. 2, 1999, transcript, Mississippi Oral History Program, University of Southern Mississippi

Rhee, Jeannie. "In Black and White: Chinese in the Mississippi Delta." *Journal of Supreme Court History: Yearbook of the Supreme Court Historical Society* (1994): 117-132.

Rummel, George A, III. "The Delta Chinese: An Exploratory Study in Assimilation." MA thesis, University of Mississippi (1966).

Rutkoff, Peter, and Scott, Will. "Preaching the Blues: The Mississippi Delta of Muddy Waters." *Kenyon Review*, Spring, 2005.

Schneider, Mary Jo and Schneider, William M. "A structural analysis of the Chinese grocery store in the Mississippi Delta." In *Visions and Revisions: Ethnohistoric Perspectives on Southern Culture, edited by* G. Sabo III and W. M. Schneider, 83-97. Athens, GA.: University of Georgia Press, 1987.

Sengupta, Somini. "Delta Chinese Hang On to a Vanishing Way of Life." *Cleveland Journal,* November 1, 2000.

Shankman, Arnold. "Black on yellow: Afro-Americans view Chinese-Americans." *Phylon,* 39, 1, (1978): 1-17

Shepherd, Ted. *The Chinese of Greenville Mississippi.* Greenville, Ms. Burford Brothers Printing Company, 1999.

Sidney, Audrey Interview by Kimberly Lancaster, Feb. 4, 2000, transcript, Delta State University Oral History Archives, Cleveland Ms.

Sprigle. Ray. "Feudalism Lives on In the Delta." *Pittsburgh Post-Gazette,* Aug. 24, 1948, 1.

Sue, Sam. "Growing up in Mississippi." In *Oral Histories of First to Fourth Generation Americans from China, the Philippines, Japan, India, the Pacific Islands, Vietnam and Cambodia, edited by* J. Faung and J. Lee, 3-9. New York: New York Press, 1991.

Thornell, John. "Where East meets West at the foot of the cross: The Chinese mission church in Greenville Mississippi." Paper presented at Southeast Conference of the Association of Asian Studies, Jekyll Island, Georgia, Jan. 2003.

Thornell, John. "A Culture in Decline: The Chinese in the Mississippi Delta." *Southeast Asian Review,* 2008, 30, 196-202.

Tri-State Chinese Directory of Mississippi, Arkansas, and Tennessee. Undated, Greenwood, Ms.: Chinese Commercial Directory Service Bureau.

Wilson, Charles R. *Chinese in Mississippi: An Ethnic People in a Biracial Society,* http://mshistory.k12.ms.us/index.php?id=86 Accessed Sept. 1, 2007.

Wing, Luck. Interview by Kimberly Lancaster, 1 March 2000.transcript, Delta State University Oral History Archives, Cleveland, Ms.

Wing, Mae. Interview by Kimberly Lancaster. March 1, 2000, transcript, Delta State University Oral History Archives, Cleveland, Ms.

Wong, Frances. Interview by Kimberly Lancaster and Jennifer Mitchell, Jan. 19, 2000, transcript, Delta State University Oral History Archives, Cleveland, Ms.

Wong, Helen. *Through my eyes: A family history.* Unpublished, 2007.

Wong, Jade Snow. *Fifth Chinese Daughter.* Seattle: University of Washington Press, 1945.

Woo. Lillie. Interview by Kimberly Lancaster and Jennifer Mitchell, Feb. 14, 2000, transcript, Delta State University Oral History Archives, Cleveland, Ms.

Yee, Alfred. *Shopping at Giant Foods: Chinese American Supermarkets in Northern California.* Seattle: University of Washington Press, 2003.

Index

Errata

p. 62   It was mistakenly reported that Joe Young achieved the rank of Colonel in China. However, he was never in the military.

Made in the USA
Charleston, SC
11 September 2011